University Research on International Affairs

Studies in
Universities and World Affairs—

AMERICAN COLLEGE LIFE AS EDUCATION IN WORLD OUTLOOK
Howard E. Wilson

FOREIGN STUDENTS AND HIGHER EDUCATION
IN THE UNITED STATES
Cora Du Bois

THE UNIVERSITY, THE CITIZEN, AND WORLD AFFAIRS
Cyril O. Houle and Charles A. Nelson

TRAINING OF SPECIALISTS IN INTERNATIONAL RELATIONS
C. Dale Fuller

INTERNATIONAL RELATIONS IN INSTITUTIONS OF HIGHER
EDUCATION IN THE SOUTH
Fred Cole

UNIVERSITY RESEARCH ON INTERNATIONAL AFFAIRS
John Gange

WORLD AFFAIRS AND THE COLLEGE CURRICULUM
Richard N. Swift

AMERICAN UNIVERSITIES IN WORLD AFFAIRS:
A GENERAL REPORT
Howard E. Wilson and Francis J. Brown

University
Research on
International
Affairs

JOHN GANGE

Director, Review and Development Department
The Asia Foundation

AMERICAN COUNCIL ON EDUCATION · *Washington, D. C.*

*Prepared for the Carnegie Endowment for International Peace;
published by the American Council on Education*

FOREWORD

WHEN the Carnegie Endowment for International Peace planned a series of eight studies on universities and world affairs, it was obvious that one of them should deal with research in the international field. A critical survey of the academic setting and general conditions confronting modern research was sought, rather than an inventory of current research which would inevitably be but a temporary contribution. Accordingly, it became essential to enlist for the study an author who could write with the detachment and the authority of a senior practitioner.

To this task John Gange has brought an unusually wide experience. In the nine years that followed his graduation from Stanford University in 1932, he engaged in further study and in teaching on both east and west coasts. The succeeding eight years found him in Washington with the Department of State and the Economic Cooperation Administration. From 1949 to 1957 he was director of the Woodrow Wilson School of Foreign Affairs at the University of Virginia; it was toward the close of this service in Charlottesville that he conducted the research and completed the manuscript for this volume.

In addition to these responsibilities, the author has been a consultant to government agencies, has been executive director of the American Political Science Association, and has been connected in various capacities with other organizations such as the Social Science Foundation, the Asia Foundation, and the Social Science Research Council. He has written on topics ranging from "Refugee Settlement in the Dominican Republic" to "The Secretariat Function." The insights gained from this variety of experience and association give weight to his observations on the problems of contemporary research.

The volume is a frank and thoughtful appraisal of the diffi-

culties attending the conduct of research, whether engaged in by
a solitary professor remote from his source material or by large
research centers. As such it will be of interest to teachers and
administrators throughout higher education—whether their concern is in the international or any other field—for all are
concerned with the advancement of knowledge and the strengthening of teaching through stimulating research. While the opinions expressed are those of the author and not of the Carnegie
Endowment, the Endowment can testify to the serious attention
that these opinions deserve.

> JOSEPH E. JOHNSON, *President*
> *Carnegie Endowment for International Peace*

EDITOR'S PREFACE

EXAMINATION of the interrelations between universities and world affairs inevitably involves scrutiny of academic research on international questions. The discovery of new knowledge is as urgent for the conduct of international relations as it is characteristic of the functions of universities. Research is the foundation on which a new study or discipline, such as international affairs, rises. In recent years emphasis on research in all fields has been accented in academic life; we are in a particularly research-minded age.

Such facts as these make the topic of this volume unusually important and timely. The volume itself is an outgrowth of a study pursued during the past decade by the Carnegie Endowment for International Peace. Concerned with the impact of world affairs on American academic life and with the importance of the role of colleges and universities in serving the United States in the formulation and operation of foreign policy, the Endowment began exploratory studies in this field. Between 1950 and 1954 a widely scattered group of colleges and universities undertook, in cooperation with the Endowment, analyses and appraisals of their activities and resources bearing on world affairs. The surveys were individually planned for each campus, and ranged widely over such topics as curricular adjustment, reception of foreign students, activities in adult education, training of specialists in international relations, research, and the extracurricular enterprises of students bearing on world affairs. Some sixty institutions completed surveys and prepared reports, which were mimeographed for limited distribution. Regional conferences were held for participating institutions. As a final result of the entire program, a series of topical studies was undertaken dealing with matters revealed as important and interrelated. Those studies—of which this is one—are now appearing as volumes in the series "Studies in Universities and World Affairs," published for the Carnegie Endowment by the American Council on Education. As indicated on an introductory page of this volume, this is the sixth such study to be published in the series, and two additional volumes are yet to be issued.

The authors of these various volumes have been asked to use the data of the institutional surveys undertaken in the Endowment program simply as starting points in treating their topics. Each author has explored available material on his subject and has dealt with the subject as he himself desired. This book on university research on international affairs, then, is not simply a report on the surveys made, but is a competent specialist's analysis of one phase of the wide-ranging interrelations of higher education and world affairs.

Particularly in this volume on research has it been necessary to go beyond the institutional self-surveys, for those surveys revealed neglect and uncertainty respecting research, particularly in the smaller colleges. Most of the reports on the surveys emphasized the importance of research, expressed the desire to do more of it, and revealed the paucity of worthy research enterprises in most institutions. Mr. Gange's volume throws light on matters which seem to bother the academic conscience. The author might simply have written a substantive analysis and critique of the academic research on international affairs which has been produced in this country in recent years. He might have written an interpretative essay on the nature and problems of research in this field. That he has chosen to deal, on the basis of his experience and observation, with the relation of research to the understanding of world affairs, with the administrative setting of research in academic institutions, with the relative merits of individual and group research, with the problems of access to materials, and with the functional rise of research findings is fortunate. Mr. Gange writes as a competent specialist who has served with distinction in governmental and academic posts and is now engaged in the staff work of an important foundation. His volume opens up a subject with which universities, governments, and individual scholars are likely to be increasingly concerned.

HOWARD E. WILSON

January 6, 1958

PREFACE

A STUDY of research in international affairs requires first of all a definition. International affairs includes, in the most general sense, the unfolding and the course of relations among nation-states in the dimensions of time and space. Second, this subject includes the beliefs, attitudes, actions, and aspirations of groups of people which may transcend, or fall short of, strictly national geographic and political boundaries; and the people may be greater in number than the population of any one state (for example, Moslems) or less in number than the total population of even the one state in which they reside (for example, native Germans in prewar Czechoslovakia or native Cypriots in contemporary Cyprus). Third, the study of international affairs may properly include the study of developments within states which are of substantial influence (past, present, or potential) on the beliefs and actions of responsible leaders and governing groups within these states, especially where subsequent actions of the state are of major importance among the family of nations.

Fourth, research in international relations very properly embraces the study of institutions (such as international law and procedures for the pacific settlement of international disputes, concepts and practices in international trade, finance, development, and so on); of organizations composed of representatives of national groups at the governmental (or semigovernmental) level; and of individuals, especially those whose efforts to ameliorate international friction and to advance international cooperation and harmony, or contrariwise, have been outstanding. Fifth, it is increasingly clear that the study of international affairs must be directed also to the behavior of man individually and men in organized societies as well as to the record of the relations between groups and between nations. The general beliefs and

ideologies which seem to motivate societies and nation-states, and
the institutions, procedures, organizations, and persons figuring
in internationally significant national actions are in a real sense
the root of international relations. The relations of states increasingly seem to be comprehensible only if the nature of man himself is more fully understood.

Last, the impact of the developments in the natural sciences
and technology on man and his natural environment have had
an increasingly important role in international affairs. This area
is the newest—and as yet almost untouched—branch of the study
of international affairs. The impact and consequences for international affairs of new forms of energy, new materials, new
weapons, and new ways of keeping more people alive for a longer
life span are increasingly significant subjects for research and
teaching.

The six-sided picture of international relations which has been
sketched above goes beyond some standard concepts of the field,
but it is apparent that the field is broadening out, and must
broaden beyond the older quadrivium of diplomatic history,
international law and organization, international politics (including concepts of nationalism, imperialism, and other "isms"), and
international commercial and financial relations. "The focus of
attention [for the student of international relations] must be on
intergovernmental relations and all things which affect them."[1]
Because of the ramifications of the last phrase in the previous
sentence, it has seemed to some that "international relations" was
too narrow a term, belonging more appropriately to the first
thought in the quoted sentence rather than to the whole sentence.
The term international affairs seems broader in scope and depth
than "international relations," and henceforth it will be used in
this report as an indication of the enlargement of this area of
knowledge and research without suggesting that all of man's
life and living come within its purview.

[1] Grayson Kirk in *The Study of International Relations* (New York: Council
on Foreign Relations, 1947), p. 9. I have applied Professor Kirk's thought to
the international relations "field" to describe the new branches of study.

This study is concerned with university exploration of these aspects of international affairs. There are more than eighteen hundred colleges and universities in the United States, and thousands of academicians are associated with these institutions. In most instances the research being done at colleges and universities is being done by persons who have some academic status as faculty members, teaching or research assistants, or the specially employed staff of an identifiable research organization under the jurisdiction of the administrative authorities of the institution. It is the research activities of these persons—primarily the "working conditions," so to speak, of these persons—which have been studied for this report.

The research being done by graduate students as candidates for advanced degrees figures only incidentally in this study. The research being done by agencies wholly contracted to United States government research, even if situated at academic institutions and directed by academicians, has not been included in the scope of this report. This research has been excluded because the academic connection is as often as not coincidental with some personal connection (not an institutional one) and because the research done usually does not enter into the stream of public knowledge through introduction into classrooms, scholarly jounals, professional meetings, and public addresses, or trade publications—all of which are the normal outlets for academic research.

From the beginning of this investigation into research in international affairs at American colleges and universities no effort has been made to prepare a catalogue or an analysis of research projects in progress or planned. This has not been a bibliographical nor an evaluative inventory-taking project. The Carnegie Endowment for International Peace in years past[2] devoted an issue (normally in December[3]) of its publication, *International Con-*

[2] In 1947, 1948, 1949, and 1950.

[3] The 1947 report appeared in the January 1948 issue of *International Conciliation.* In 1952, the Endowment published this annual bibliography as a book with an introductory essay by Frederick S. Dunn on the characteristics of the research projects reported in 1952.

ciliation, to the subject of "Current Research in International Affairs." Other specialists in this field of study have from time to time performed a similar service in reviewing and reporting who is doing what research on international affairs. The Department of State through its External Research Staff also has endeavored in recent years to keep a running inventory of current research in international relations at academic and other research centers. For more specialized purposes there have also been surveys, inventories, and activity files on specialized and technical personnel by other governmental and international agencies which have uncovered and sometimes reported the research activity of this kind.

At the level of doctoral dissertation subjects there have been annual or periodic listings in the professional journals of the disciplines most extensively concerned with international affairs. Foundations, professional organizations, and specialized learned societies have also prepared inventories from time to time on various aspects of research in international affairs (for example, on area studies, on interdisciplinary research, and the like), and their reports have had general distribution, or at least they have been available to administrators and those persons who have specialized research interests related to the fields covered by these special inventories. Another reason for not attempting an additional inventory of recent research is the availability of abundant current reporting of research to be found in the book review and "news and notes" sections of several professional and learned journals and some trade publications which touch this broad field of international affairs.

No one with a serious interest in research in international affairs need be uninformed on what research is being published nor even be uninformed on the broad outlines of many current research projects which envisage future publication.

In the belief that there is no present urgent need for inventories or catalogues of published and ongoing research, this report focuses instead on what might be called the *administra-*

tive setting for research in international affairs in American colleges and universities. Some references to current research work have been made for purposes illustrative of the topics raised under the "administrative" rubric. The only major departure from this plan is a venture in discussing what might well be undertaken by researchers in international affairs.

The "administrative setting for research" has been divided into the following categories: (*a*) The status of research in international affairs in American colleges and universities; (*b*) the characteristics of administrative support for research in colleges and universities; (*c*) the organization, methods, and techniques for research and attitudes toward research in international affairs in colleges and universities; (*d*) the problem of access to materials essential to realistic research in international affairs; (*e*) the outlets for academic research and the uses of academic research; and (*f*) areas which need more research and more administrative support for research than is generally being provided. In all these categories this report makes no claims to being either exhaustive or definitive. The objective rather has been to point up type problems or achievements, to note the general features of development in this conceptual framework of the administrative setting, and to venture some conclusions and suggestions in each of the categories covered.

It is hoped that the report will be read primarily by college and university administrators, including trustees, and by alumni or friends of institutions of higher learning who have helped finance the high costs of teaching and research. It is hoped also that young scholars will find the report useful as a general guide to a field of possible research. Established scholars in this field will probably find the report too brief and too sketchy, but the author has assumed that these specialists are quite adequately informed on the subject of this report already. In fact much of what is in the report came from the author's conversations with these scholars and the administrators who were interviewed.

The institutional self-surveys undertaken by over sixty American colleges and universities regarding their programs directed to, or related to, the study of world affairs produced very little data on the subject of research in international affairs. Many of the institutions undertaking these self-surveys made no mention of research, either because there was no research in international affairs on their campuses or because this aspect of their total activity was overlooked. It was necessary for me to visit as many institutions as my time would permit and to gather information and opinions by interviews, correspondence, and from published materials.

Many academic and government colleagues have provided me with information and have asked stimulating questions in reply to my questions. I held up this manuscript, first written in the spring of 1956, until I could review it with a competitively selected group of participants in the Social Science Research Council's Summer Research Training Institute on Current Research in International Affairs in 1956, of which I was the director. I am deeply grateful to all my colleagues for their generous assistance. In gathering data for this report I have also had the able assistance of Mr. William E. Dorrill, Miss Elizabeth Hatcher, and Miss Neela Sattanathan, then graduate students at the University of Virginia. None of these persons is responsible for the conclusions I drew from some of the data they helped me collect. These evaluations are my own responsibility, but I am confident that my colleagues and assistants helped me to better judgments.

JOHN GANGE

August 1, 1956

CONTENTS

CONTENTS

1. Research in International Affairs at American Colleges and Universities

Attempt the end, and never stand to doubt;
Nothing's so hard but search will find it out.

Robert Herrick, *Seek and Find*

IN THE process of reviewing the institutional self-survey reports for the project on Universities and World Affairs, described in the Editor's Preface, and in the course of interviewing persons concerned with research in international affairs at academic centers, a considerable range of opinion was revealed as to the proper role of academic research in international affairs.[1]

An attitude encountered quite often regarded research as something apart from teaching, a sort of added attraction, or an added obligation, depending on the individual's general concept of teaching and research. In some cases research was regarded apparently as a side show in which the participants displayed their erudition, having somehow "stolen" time from teaching and administration to engage in these self-glorifying activities. It was not uncommon, also, to encounter the expression: "This is a teaching institution and we have little time for, and give little emphasis to, research." The same expression occurs not infrequently in applications and recommendations for Fulbright research fellowships or lecturing awards to advanced scholars and in other

[1] One of the best discussions of attitudes toward research and other normal academic duties and opportunities may be found in a chapter by Elbridge Sibley in his report on *Support for Independent Scholarships and Research* (New York: Social Science Research Council, 1951). The chapter is entitled "The Academic Environment."

comparable fellowship applications.[2] An extreme statement in this respect was made by a faculty member at a well-regarded small college who observed that emphasis on research was regarded as a threat to teaching, which was the sole purpose of that institution.

On the other side of this controversy are many who believe that research, particularly research for publication, is certainly the main function of a university and that even college faculties should regard research as being as important as teaching. In many universities much emphasis is placed upon scholarly research and publication, and appointments and promotions are largely determined by evidence of research interests and achievements. Individual departments usually report their research to their deans and presidents, and sometimes report even more publicly the gross annual output of research. In certain cases where everything, from book notes through book reviews, articles, monographs, and books, is listed and tallied separately, the whole activity often takes on the aspect of a factory accounting to its management and stockholders for the year's output of various kinds of products fabricated by them. Exponents of this research emphasis have been known to chide new faculty members if they loiter in the halls talking to students between classes or if they permit seminars or preceptorials to go beyond the scheduled time, because time so "wasted" could be used to write a few paragraphs. And paragraphs add up to articles, which if properly hung together, can be made into books. The ultimate in this view of course is the "ideal" institution which some faculty members seek: a limitless library, ample funds for assistants and other research needs, generous faculty salaries, and no students.

This controversy has been a part of university life since the days of Peter Abelard and others like him, who have been torn between expounding existing knowledge and opinion as teachers

[2] It is worth noting that there is a remarkable coincidence of this kind of comment with a blank page for the listing of "research and publications." How often this generalization about the role of research versus teaching is an excuse for a specific failure to do *any* research is a matter of conjecture.

and exploring the frontiers for new knowledge, or testing existing knowledge, as researchers. To further harass the academicians there has also developed since Abelard's day a burden of administrative chores of almost countless variation and of a seemingly more and more time-consuming character. The editor of a journal often devoted to matters on international affairs once suggested that there should be three ladders for appointment and promotion in rank and pay: one for teaching, one for research, and one for administration. There are many who would subscribe to this trichotomy; others, however, might qualify it by arguing that all three elements ought to enter equally into the evaluation of an academician's ability and performance. Exponents of these respective three emphases in the academic life sometimes carry their argument to the point of urging that graduate schools be so organized as to produce teachers, or researchers, or administrators.

There is a middle ground between the schools of thought on teaching versus research (or teaching versus research versus administration) which holds that a member of a college or university faculty has several obligations as well as opportunities. By definition ("instructor," "lecturer," or "professor") he is expected to be qualified and eager to lead students through an important stage of the greatest adventure in life—learning about man, his environment, his life on earth, and his possible destiny. But if teachers were to do no more than expound what is already known or believed, then unbearable stagnation in human affairs would have set in long ago and the prospect for the living would be as dull and dreary as some of the unchanging "heavens" men have dreamed up for their dead.

Surely a teacher must persist in his own learning, which is primarily by way of research, if he is to make his teaching worth the effort for himself and his students. And he ought to publish his research for the great community around him which, often unwittingly yet unavoidably, responds to the new knowledge which is revealed every day. Helping to bring more satisfaction and achievement out of the educative process by better administration at the college and university level is also an obligation which every college teacher ought to assume, for he is otherwise partially parasitical on the body which makes his preferred professional activities possible. Beyond the campus lie still other obligations to the small and great communities of men of which, by choice and by necessity, the teacher is a part, and unless he chooses the hermit's existence, he must contribute to the requirements of these groups which help to give him a normal life.

All these and no less should be the framework for the activity of an academician and for the evaluation of the work and the professional worth of any academician.[3] Each man, of course, will have some one emphasis among all of these requirements, but all of them should be a part of his pattern of living.[4]

Research in International Affairs

The study of international affairs is to a considerable degree in its infancy. At least as an identifiable academic subject it is a very recent arrival into the company of subjects or disciplines which men have studied and expounded systematically for centuries. International relations as a subject touches the whole gamut of human affairs and also the responses and limitations on action imposed by the natural environment of man, by man's scientific developments and knowledge of the earth, life, and cosmic sciences, and by man's technology.[5] To give coherence and

[3] For a good measuring chart for the performance of college faculties see E. Kent Springer, "Criteria for Advancement and Promotion of the Teaching Staff," *Higher Education*, III (Jan. 15, 1951), 117–18.

[4] For a good recent statement on the role of college teachers in society see the statement by Dr. Charles W. Cole, president of Amherst College in the *Amherst Alumni News*, July 1955.

See also *Higher Education in a Decade of Decision,* Report of the Educational Policies Commission of the National Education Association of the United States and the American Association of School Administrators (Washington: The Commission, 1957), pp. 63–70.

[5] See Geoffrey L. Goodwin (ed.), *The University Teaching of International Relations,* a report of the International Studies Conference (New York: Macmillan Co., 1951). See also C. A. W. Manning, "General Report on the Teaching of International Relations," for Experts' Meeting on the Teaching of the Social Sciences called by Unesco on Sept. 16–19, 1952 ([Paris?]: Unesco's S.S. Conf. 6.1, August 1952).

the quality of a discipline to this sprawling range of subject matter is an undertaking of immense proportions and difficulty, if not of considerable presumption and audacity, on the part of its students and teachers. In the circumstances of an emerging discipline with ill-defined boundaries and unexplored depths of subject matter, there is a pre-eminent need for abundant research (a) as the foundation for teaching this subject, (b) for application of general principles and knowledge to specific operational needs and action situations in governments, and (c) for guidance for the researchers themselves in this area of human affairs. There is a need also for research directed to the problem of informing the public in such a manner and to such a degree that serious citizens may be better equipped to comprehend the course of their nation's foreign relations. The trained scholars in international affairs are employed almost entirely by academic institutions and governmental agencies, but a few do find employment in the various media devoted directly to informing the general public. The fruits of academic research are, therefore, of wide utility.

In the United States today there are many thousands of persons engaged full or part time in the serious study of international affairs. The great majority of these persons are in governmental agencies and in the main they are preoccupied with operational research: digging out the data needed, or possibly useful, in wrestling with immediate or emerging action problems. In the Department of State, in the Foreign Service of the United States, in the Central Intelligence Agency, in the National Security Agency, in the intelligence and psychological warfare branches of the military departments, in the Legislative Reference Service of the Library of Congress, on the staffs of numerous congressional committees and executive branch interdepartmental committees and councils, there is a vast busyness in searching into international affairs.[6] It is doubtful if even in wartime there were so many American public servants searching the world over

[6] See the report of the Commission on Organization of the Executive Branch of the Government (second Hoover Commission) on *Intelligence Activities* (Washington: Government Printing Office).

for information which might contribute to the shaping of policies and programs serving the national interests of the United States in its foreign relations. Much of what is studied by these government workers has come from nongovernmental researchers in this country and in other countries of the world, and government agencies seem to be especially interested in sharply focused studies by scholars who have an eye to operational problems.

Private, nonacademic research centers in the United States have also contributed significantly for many years to the available knowledge and opinion about international affairs. Groups like the Council on Foreign Relations, the Woodrow Wilson Foundation, the Foreign Policy Association, the Institute of Pacific Relations, the Carnegie Endowment for International Peace, the World Peace Foundation, the Twentieth Century Fund, the Brookings Institution, and the National Planning Association are outstanding examples of such private but nonacademic centers for research. They have carried on research, or have financed others to do so, or have facilitated research by maintaining excellent research libraries or by publishing documents in convenient collections or in journals or other periodicals helpful to researchers.[7] It should be noted that these organizations have drawn heavily on academic scholars for much of their research work.

Since World War II some new nonacademic private research organizations have developed which have done extensive research or have facilitated research in international affairs. Examples in this category are the RAND Corporation, the Committee for Economic Development, the Public Affairs Institute, the Middle East Institute, the American Universities Field Staff, headquartered in New York, and the Mid-European Studies Center in New York. There are numerous others, but these are prominent examples of this more recent development in research centers

---

[7] For brief accounts of the activities of these groups (except the National Planning Association) see *Institutes of International Affair* (New York: Carnegie Endowment for International Peace, 1953).

concerned with public affairs and especially with international affairs.

There are many individuals who are not attached to any organization in any formal connection who do research in international affairs. Some are former government employees or retired military officers; others are professional free-lance researchers and writers.[8] These men are distinct from the numerous company of those who have been busy writing their memoirs and those who have been reporters of the day-to-day developments in international affairs.

Research in Colleges and Universities

In the academic institutions there is considerable research activity. It ranges from a barely discernible research interest on the part of some teachers to a very conspicuous amount of research and publication on the part of others. Among some two hundred institutions visited by the author during the past eight years this wide range of activity has been verified again and again, year after year. It should be noted, too, that even where there is not much activity in actual research in international affairs, there is an interest in what has been, or is being, done elsewhere and usually there is a desire to do more research than is actually being done. Research-mindedness has probably increased in recent years due to the conspicuous work of a few big research centers.

In many small colleges, especially those remote from cosmopolitan centers with their superior library resources and other good facilities for research, it is fair to say that research in international affairs in the strict sense of the word hardly exists. Teaching loads are usually very heavy in these institutions, fifteen hours being the common requirement, with sometimes more expected. To this teaching burden may be added other duties such as counseling students, supervising residence halls or dining halls,

---

[8] Notable in this category are men like Herbert Feis, James P. Warburg; Thomas K. Finletter, Walter Lippmann, James Burnham, William H. Chamberlin, Hanson Baldwin, and others.

conducting convocations, and organizing and directing a host of extracurricular activities, of which only one or two may be related to international affairs. Administrative duties, faculty committees, community services, extension teaching or extra night courses, and other comparable activities absorb much of the time and the energy of the faculty members of many academic institutions.[9]

It is difficult to see how many teachers in such situations could do more research than they do without extraordinary effort and rigid discipline over the few precious hours of free time which they can find in their crowded routine. Part of the difficulty lies in the administrative arrangements for, and the attitudes toward, research at such institutions—and these will be discussed in the next chapter. Part of the deficiency, however, probably lies in the persons themselves. Many of these heavily burdened teachers probably could do some useful research in international relations even in locations with limited facilities for research if they would use more imagination in choosing research topics adapted to their situations, and if they had been better trained to be versatile and flexible in their research methods. Research on public opinion studies or the role of interest groups, analyses of the "image" of the outer world held by Americans, the effect of education and foreign travel on changes in these images are a few examples of the kinds of research which could be done in any college. Most college teachers have not been properly trained, however, to do this research.

In the average institutions—if there is such a thing as an "average" institution of higher learning out of the hundreds of such which claim that function in America—there is usually some fair amount of research activity in international affairs. In

---

[9] The findings of a recent survey of research and teaching in international affairs in Southern colleges and universities bear out this generalization with respect to research activity: Fred Cole, *International Relations in Institutions of Higher Education in the South* (Washington: American Council on Education, 1958), pp. 113–15.

the political science departments[10] of these average institutions there is usually one man (and sometimes two or more) who is not only teaching a course on international affairs but is also actively engaged in research on pertinent subject matter for which he has a special interest or some background experience. Also in history departments and economics departments there will be one or more men searching into some aspect of international affairs which is particularly germane to their discipline and their teaching. Occasionally, but much less often, there will be researchers in international affairs in departments of sociology, anthropology, geography, psychology, and education. If the institution has a law school, there may be at least one man doing research in some of the legal aspects of international affairs, and in graduate schools of business or in public administration bureaus the same will be true for matters of trade and finance or public affairs management.

Even in these average institutions, however, including some very good colleges and universities, the actual amount of active and vigorous research in international affairs does not appear large when seen from the point of view of the available—or potential—personnel for research. As will be noted later, there is a considerable amount of research being done, but the point ventured here is that many more people might be active in research than is now the case.

The institutional self-surveys prepared under the Carnegie Endowment project on Universities in World Affairs bear out this statement on the paucity of research at many academic centers. Out of over sixty such institutional surveys many make almost no reference to research. Even the most detailed report[11] has only

[10] There are over three hundred such departments devoted solely to political science or to political science and history combined. There are more departments of history, as it is an older discipline.

[11] "The State University of Iowa and World Affairs," *Universities and World Affairs*, Document No. 80 (Mimeographed; Carnegie Endowment for International Peace, 1955).

Also see Appendix (p. 130) for other comments from institutional reports of self-surveys.

one page on "research bearing on world affairs" out of 108 pages of text on the institution's program on world affairs. Indicative of the proportion of persons reporting research in international affairs at this institution are the following figures: "Of the 454 respondents [to a questionnaire distributed to faculty members asking for a listing of their publications on international affairs and for information concerning the supervision of relevant research on the part of graduate students] only 32 provided information. Fifteen of the 32 were in the humanities (history, literature, and foreign languages), seven in the social sciences (economics, geography, political science, and sociology), five in education, two in religion, and one each in geology, journalism, and men's physical education."[12] The authors of this institutional survey report note that the responses to their questionnaire ought to be qualified by the fact that "much research done on the campus on social and scientific problems relates to human affairs, but is not generally thought of as 'world affairs' as defined for the purposes of our investigation." They also note that "the questionnaire was faulty in that it did not provide to faculty members a clear definition of the kind of research on which a report was expected; in fact it is doubtful whether a definition could be devised which would produce reliable results when interpreted by several hundred different persons."[13]

In the last half of the quotation above lies a possible explanation for the very limited amount of information on research in international affairs to be found in these institutional self-surveys. No one has been able to set the boundaries of the subject of international affairs in such a clear and concise fashion as to avoid widely differing interpretations by hundreds of people. As noted

---

[12] *Ibid.*, p. 98. In the Southern survey by Fred Cole referred to earlier, it was found that international affairs research was more commonly carried on (by a slight margin) in departments of history than in departments of political science, due probably to there being more of the former departments than the latter. See also Fred Cole, *International Relations in Institutions of Higher Education in the South* (Washington: American Council on Education, 1958).

[13] *Ibid.*, p. 98.

in earlier pages of this report, the subject defies delimitation unless one capitulates to the proponents of the definition that international affairs has the dimensions of all human affairs qualified by the requirement that there must be some evidence, or possibility, that the conduct and consequences of these human affairs affect the relations of groups of people living in identifiable nation-states. On this very broad definition there would no doubt be much more research reported for this purpose.

It may be worth noting at this point a rather comparable inquiry made by the Legislative Reference Service of the Library of Congress for a congressional committee intent on a "down-to-date survey of United States resources in the way of organized research facilities and activities in the general field of contemporary international affairs." This inquiry was sent to colleges, universities, and other established, nongovernmental research centers on June 15, 1953, with a letter from the senior specialist in international relations of the Legislative Reference Service.[14] The inquiry asked for data on "programs of organized research covering any phase or aspect of contemporary international affairs or any current international or foreign situation." The response to this inquiry was so negligible and the answers were so inadequate that the staff of the Legislative Reverence Service made no effort to compile the data. Of those few colleges and universities which did reply to the questionnaire, the common observation was that they had no organized research arrangements.[15]

Where then is the bulk of academic-based research in international affairs being done? The answer to this question is probably like the answer to a comparable question on research in the natural sciences, some other social sciences, and perhaps the humanities also. The great bulk of the research is done at a

[14] The inquiry appears to have been the outgrowth of some questions raised in the hearings on the Library of Congress budget for 1954. See Legislative-Judiciary Appropriations for 1954, *Hearings*, Committee on Appropriations of the House of Representatives (subcommittee), 83rd Cong., 1st Sess. (Washington: Government Printing Office), pp. 176–79.

[15] Conversation with Dr. Halford L. Hoskins of the Legislative Reference Service several months after the project was initiated.

relatively few large universities and in special research institutes attached, in varying degrees of organic integration, to these large institutions. Judged by published output and by the participation of their personnel at professional meetings, it is safe to say that about one-sixth of all institutions having departments of political science or specialized departments of international affairs are doing the major portion of the campus-based research in international affairs. This is a group of roughly forty to fifty institutions, constituting less than 6 percent of the membership (763 members in 1958) of the Association of American Colleges. This group of institutions includes all the members of the Association of American Universities,[16] and some ten or twelve additional centers.

This determination is based on various published reports of current research in international affairs[17] at American colleges and universities and by the author's observations of, and experience during the postwar years with, the locus of research activity in this field. A study of professional journals and of published bibliographies reveals that the persons attached to these prominent institutions are producing the bulk of the published research in this field. A review also of foundation grants in recent years shows that by far the greatest proportion of this kind of financial aid is also being given primarily to this small group of institutions and to a lesser degree to the other centers for the study of international affairs.

How Much Research Is Being Done?

To ask this question and to attempt a complete answer is, of course, to venture the impossible. No one knows how much re-

16 See *Journal of Proceedings and Addresses* of the annual meetings of the association for a list of members.

17 Confirmation of these selections can be found, for example, in reports on current research in international affairs in the January and December, 1948, and in the December, 1949 and 1950, issues of *International Conciliation* published by the Carnegie Endowment for International Peace. The fifth report appeared under the title *Current Research in International Affairs*, with Introduction by Frederick S. Dunn (New York: The Endowment, 1952).

search is being done any more than anyone knows how much thinking is being done. One can, however, look at published research in international affairs and compare it with published research in some other fields and thereby get some idea of the magnitude of the research which is brought to public view in this field. A cautionary note should be sounded here with respect to the adequacy of publication as a test for the amount of research being done in international affairs.

As noted earlier, research and teaching ought not to be thought of as wholly separate undertakings. To teach anything, knowledge must first be revealed, or uncovered; it must be organized in a form suitable for presentation to students; and it ought to be subjected to continuing analysis and criticism. Many a good teacher does research and is research-minded in the broad sense of the word. In the preparation of his course materials, syllabi, lectures, problem assignments and supporting readings, thesis and dissertation guidance and review, and other comparable academic functions, he does much research which may never glisten from a neatly printed page or be bound between hard covers with a satisfying title and the author's surname on the shelfback. Countless students and scholars have known great teachers whose published output was slight but whose role in the educative process was immense. There is a derogatory phrase sometimes used by ineffective teachers about a colleague noted for his good teaching: "He may be a good teacher but he is not a great scholar."

The author of this report vigorously eschews any such invidious concept or attitude, for he believes that this kind of judgment is beyond the competence of any single person to make. There is much more subtlety in the phrase "a contribution to knowledge" than most of us realize. It is doubtful, indeed, that research must be published before the effort expended can be called "research."

As soon as one begins a quantitative measurement of the amount of research published in the field of international affairs, one trips—again—over the definition of the field. Compilations of research in international affairs in progress, or recently published, reveal a wide variation in criteria on what to include and what to exclude.[18] One must be sympathetic, then, with any investigator or author who ventures into this no man's land where there are certain to be snipers from many disciplines who believe or do *not* believe that such and such research properly comes under the expansive umbrella of international affairs.

Judging by (a) the description of research projects reported for doctoral dissertations;[19] (b) by the research papers read at professional meetings of political scientists, historians, and economists; (c) by projects proposed in connection with Fulbright applications, Guggenheim Foundation and Social Science Research Council research grants, and the Ford Foundation Overseas Fellowship Program (to mention only a few sources for individual research awards), it is clear that a considerable amount of research is planned or in progress or recently completed in the field of international affairs.

A study made by Claude E. Hawley and Lewis A. Dexter of "research in progress in political science departments of American universities in the spring of 1950"[20] produced some data on the

[18] Compare, for example, the annual reports by the Carnegie Endowment, cited in footnote 17, with bibliographies prepared by such groups as the Council on Foreign Relations of New York and the Royal Institute of International Affairs of London. See also the very wide range of subject matter listed in the "External Research" series put out by the External Research Staff, Office of Intelligence Research, U.S. Department of State. In the case of the Carnegie Endowment reports and the State Department reports the determination of what was in international affairs rested initially, and rather largely, with the institutions and individuals filling out the respective periodic questionnaires. In the case of the council and the institute the selection was more narrowly controlled.

[19] *Doctoral Dissertations Accepted by American Universities* (New York: H. W. Wilson Co., annually, 1933–34 to 1954–55. See also annual listings of doctoral dissertation topics in the *American Political Science Review,* occasional listings in the *American Historical Review* and the *American Economic Review,* and specialized reports on doctoral dissertations such as *A Bibliography of Unpublished Doctoral Dissertations and Masters Theses Dealing with Governments, Politics, and International Relations of Latin America,* by Harry Kantor for the Committee on Latin American Affairs of the American Political Science Association (Gainesville, Fla.: Inter-American Bibl. & Library Assoc., 1953).

[20] Hawley and Dexter, "Recent Political Science Research in American Universities," *American Political Science Review,* XLVI (June 1952), 470.

relative position of research in international relations and the other, perhaps narrower, branches of that whole discipline. The data they analyzed came from replies sent in by 75 chairmen of political science departments (out of 112 questionnaires sent out); of these 75, 14 reported that no research was being conducted in their departments. Despite the fact that only 61 graduate departments of political science replied to the questionnaire, the authors of this study believe that "at least 75 percent of the research being conducted by or in departments of political science was reported and subsequently analyzed."[21]

After noting the difficulty of categorizing political science according to fields, Hawley and Dexter divided the research areas of political science into ten areas and then distributed the reported research projects among these categories, sometimes entering one project in more than one classification. For the purposes of the present report on research in international relations the following data from the Hawley-Dexter study is relevant: Out of 797 research projects tabulated in the ten classifications, the area of international relations had 308 entries, being thereby the largest single concentration.[22] If one adds comparative politics and government with 34 entries and then turns to the itemized breakdowns in other categories (there was no breakdown for comparative politics and government) to note studies in or closely related to international affairs, it is apparent that some type of international relations research made up over half of all these 797 reported projects.[23] The authors note that their study confirmed Charles E. Merriam's earlier observation on the increasing importance of international relations as a subject of inquiry.[24]

[21] *Ibid.* This opinion is supported by other data regarding the locus of major research activity in universities.

[22] *Ibid.*, p. 472.

[23] *Ibid.* This increase over the 308 plus 34 is achieved by adding those research projects of an "international" character which had been entered in "area studies," p. 475; "public administration," p. 477; "studies in pressure groups, political parties, public opinion, representation, and legislation," p. 480; and "studies in political theory," p. 482.

[24] Quoted from "Political Science in the United States," in *Contemporary Political Science,* pp. 247–48, as cited by Hawley and Dexter, *op. cit.*

In a more recent survey[25] of trends in political science in America, Dwight Waldo and Gerald Nash analyzed and categorized articles appearing in five leading political science journals during selected periods of time. For the period 1952–54[26] they found that 27 percent of a total of 418 articles were in the area of international relations. The Waldo-Nash tabulation seems to have used more sharply defined categories than the Hawley-Dexter tabulation. No addition has been made of area studies or comparative government which certainly contain a sizable body of international affairs subjects, to say nothing of similarly oriented studies in public administration (especially comparative administration) and studies in political parties, pressure groups, propaganda, public opinion, and political theory. In all these areas more and more attention has been given to international or foreign area research projects.

In analyzing and categorizing book reviews published in the *American Political Science Review (APSR)* for 1952–54, Waldo and Nash found 17 percent of the books reviewed lay within their definition of international relations and 19 percent within the area of foreign and comparative government. The same qualification noted above for the articles analyzed should probably be applied to the book reviews included in their study.

With respect to both articles published and books reviewed, it is worth noting that Waldo and Nash found a very marked increase in interest (or research activity) in international relations in 1952–54 as compared with 1939–41: For articles published, the percentage went from 11 percent in 1939–41 to 27 percent in 1952–54; for books reviewed in the *APSR* the percentage in international relations went from 13 percent in 1939–41 to 17 percent in 1952–54.[27]

[25] Made for the Social Science Division of Unesco, 1955.

[26] The journals read for 1952–54 were the *American Political Science Review*, the *Journal of Politics, Political Science Quarterly, Review of Political Science,* and the *Western Political Quarterly.*

[27] Data cited here was taken from a MS of Professor Waldo's study which has since been delivered to Unesco for a study being made of trends in political science in several selected countries.

One possible explanation for the lower percentage of international affairs research published (Waldo-Nash) as compared with international affairs research projected (Hawley-Dexter) is that in the case of published research one must keep in mind the general policy of journal editors (including book review editors) to try to maintain a fairly even spread of articles and book reviews among the several areas of the discipline, for example, political science, history, and economics. This may produce a distorted picture of what is actually going on if it is seen only through the journals of national and regional political science associations.

Also, the data are based on only five general political science journals (and only four for 1939–41) and do not take into account the very considerable amount of publication of articles and book reviews in the more specialized subject journals. In the case of international affairs, for example, one would have to take note of the voluminous research published in the *American Journal of International Law, World Politics, Foreign Affairs, The Middle East Journal, International Conciliation, The Far Eastern Survey, Pacific Affairs,* and so on. The same, of course, would be true generally of other areas of political science, but not to the same extent, with the possible exception of public administration for which there are numerous specialized scholarly journals.

It was mentioned earlier that the papers read at professional and scholarly association meetings might be an indication of the amount of interest, and hence research, in international affairs. Comparisons over a period of years are difficult to make with respect to the annual meetings of the American Political Science Association because the pattern of the annual meetings was changed considerably in 1952 from what it had been previously. However, the programs for 1952, 1953, 1954, and 1955 show clearly that international affairs occupied much more of the program than its apparent proportion of being only one out of seven subdivisions for the program plan. Taking the three years 1953, 1954, and 1955, by which time the new pattern for the annual meetings was rather firmly established, one finds that 166 discussion papers were read at these three meetings and that 60 of these papers dealt with some aspect of international affairs, including the teaching and research problems in this field. This was more than one-third of all papers read—36 percent, to be exact.

What does the foregoing discussion suggest? First of all, there is the evidence that at many institutions of higher learning there is no research at all—or of any noticeable amount—in international affairs. Second, much of the research in international affairs is being done at relatively few institutions, and a very large part of it at only a very small number of institutions. Third, despite this small number of centers very actively engaged in research in international affairs, there is a growing amount of research in international affairs in relation to other branches of political science. The same conclusion could probably be established also in other fields of the social sciences such as history, anthropology, and psychology.

It may occur to some administrators who have read the foregoing discussion of current academic research in international affairs that there is no need to give additional support to this field of study. The evidence of a recent remarkable growth of interest[28] by scholars in this subject and the relative increase of the research activities in international affairs may be misleading. The state of the relations among the nations and peoples of the world today clearly argues for more adequate knowledge about these relationships and their motivations, directions, and consequences than is now possessed anywhere in the world. More research will require more researchers, if it is assumed that the presently active scholars are working at something close to their maximum efficiency.

However, other demands upon the academic community, coupled with the actual shortage of manpower in the twenty-five to thirty-five age bracket for the next decade, make it unlikely

[28] For example, see the entries under "international relations," and closely related "fields," of the listings of "primary fields of interest" in the *Directory* of the American Political Science Association for 1953 as compared with these listings in the *Directory* of the association for 1948.

that very many new young researchers will be drawn into this field in the near future. There must, therefore, be some other efforts to increase productivity in research in international affairs by improving the skills of the presently available researchers and by attracting to the field researchers now engaged in studies in other areas.

Improving Skills of Scholars Already Doing Research in International Relations

To improve the skills of scholars presently doing research calls for more extensive and expensive administrative support. That is to say, administrators must show more interest in having research done in this field, make more effort to free teachers of some of their teaching load (for example, by granting leaves of absence for research at the time teachers are given tenure appointments), support efforts to hold faculty research seminars where older scholars may provide guidance and encouragement to young scholars, and to the fullest extent possible provide money for materials, clerical help, for travel for scholars to attend professional meetings and to participate in research conferences, and for field research during summer recesses.

Outside nonacademic organizations can supplement what administrators can do in their own institutions. The Social Science Research Council faculty fellowships are an example of joint effort and support by college administrations and outside bodies to help young scholars maintain their research work during the early years of teaching. The new international relations training fellowships of the Ford Foundation (first opened to competition in the fall of 1955) are another form of aid to teachers and advanced students who want to "retool," or better, "tool up" for more productive research in international affairs. This program will not realize its worthy objectives, however, unless administrators are willing to grant leaves of absence to the young scholars who may be offered these fellowships.[29]

[29] Nine such fellowships were awarded for 1956–57.

Another device for catalyzing and improving interest and skills in research in this field is the summer workshop, or training institute. The Social Science Research Council has provided this kind of opportunity in the field of comparative government and for international affairs proper. The 1956 Summer Research Training Institute on Research in Current International Affairs provided a seven-week clinic for thirteen young researchers (average age thirty-six) to meet with a succession of outstanding research scholars in this field to study actual ongoing research projects as well as to discuss theoretical and methodological questions.[30]

More such conferences and workshops, or clinics, would help to invigorate and sharpen the research of men already well committed to this field of study. A variant of this device would be the arranging of annual summer research exercises for groups of young scholars, patterned along the lines of military war games. Participants would be located at centers rich in resources for particular kinds of research and then be assigned "positions" or "roles" for a given complex of problems and events, which could be either historical or contemporary. This device would go beyond the policy-making, problem-paper type of exercise and ought to be at least a six- to eight-week exercise. It is to be hoped that the government, as well as foundations and academic centers, will see the potential benefit to theoretical and applied research of a wider use of such devices to stimulate and train young researchers in this field.

Interesting Scholars in Other Fields To Take Up Research in International Affairs

Another means of increasing research production in the vineyard of international affairs is to attract to this area established

---

[30] This institute was held at the University of Denver, June 11 to July 27, 1956. Visiting discussion leaders were: Max Millikan, Frederick S. Dunn, Ithiel de Sola Pool, Klaus Knorr, William T. R. Fox, Gabriel Almond, Nathan Leites, and Hans Speier. The author of this report was the director of the institute.

scholars who are not now so oriented in their research. The dramatic quality of contemporary international affairs has already had some effect in this respect, and some scholars who had never worked in this field before World War II have turned their skills and interests to it since 1945. The war experience (followed by the specter of nuclear military weapons and the intensity of the cold war) and the on-and-off participation in overseas relief, development, and technical assistance programs have contributed to this process of conversion (some may consider it diversion), to the field of international affairs.

In probing with natural scientists, engineers, and social scientists the possibilities for joint conferences and year-long workshops on the theme of the impact on international affairs of new discoveries in the natural sciences and new developments in technology, the author found the scientists and engineers he interviewed to be enthusiastic about such joint endeavors. It was interesting, in fact, that scholars who had not previously been involved in international affairs research often were more concerned about the need for this kind of joint endeavor than were some of the persons specializing in international affairs.

Some of the Unesco research projects (notably the studies of international tensions) have helped to bring new scholars into the international affairs field. Fulbright awards for advanced research abroad have often served to arouse interest in international affairs problems on the part of those who first went abroad with quite different research interests. Interdisciplinary conferences have also sparked new research interests for many mature scholars. One could cite many more ways of developing this potential resource of new international affairs research, but these examples may suffice.

Conclusion

The irony in the oncoming situation for academic researchers is that we have developed a number of means to support extensive overseas- and United States–based research just at the time when it is becoming more difficult for teachers to avail themselves of these opportunities. Many of the older teachers have had considerable time away from classrooms on government work and on Fulbright fellowships or other such awards, but now they must cope with rising class enrollments and are also likely to be increasingly burdened with administrative duties. Rising enrollments are producing growing pressures on teachers to stay in their classrooms and forego the attractions and benefits of time off for research. Administrative officers seem to be increasingly reluctant to let their teachers go on leave—a contrast to the situation in the last five years when they welcomed programs like the faculty fellowships of the Fund for the Advancement of Education, if the leave was in the regular academic year.[31]

It is worth emphasizing again that the summer months may be the only time that most college teachers will have for research in the period just ahead. For this reason donors of research awards and organizers of conferences and other programs ought to give thought to this contingency and make provision for more short-term research grants. Even if it means a higher proportionate outlay of funds for travel than has been the case with the nine-month, full-year, and two-year awards for study grants and field work abroad, short-term awards will be worth while and even essential. If colleges should go on a speed-up plan through the full year and if rotating teaching assignments are adopted by administrations, then teachers might get some breaks of three or four months at times other than summer. But also if a speed-up plan is adopted, teachers could be caught in a squeeze, without any leave.

It is possible that most teachers "have had it" as far as being able to get away from their classrooms or their campuses in the

[31] One of the finest centers for the study of international affairs has already encountered difficulty in finding highly qualified persons for one of their best fellowships due to the reluctance of "home" institutions to grant leave of absence to the invitees to accept these one-year fellowships.

See also the article by Peter F. Drucker, "Will the Colleges Blow Their Tops?" *Harper's*, CCXIII, July 1956, 63–68.

next few years to do uninterrupted research for extended periods of time. A wholly inadequate supply of teachers face an oncoming deluge of students.[32] For a subject which has been growing in popularity as fast as has the field of international studies, and is likely to continue to grow, this situation is doubly unfortunate and distressing. Scholarly research may be the first casualty in the next decade, followed inexorably by a decline in good teaching, including stimulating teacher-student cooperation in exploring and searching into international affairs. Unless some changes can be made in the conditions and terms of assistance for research, there may be an increasing number of opportunities unfilled or filled by persons not regarded as very promising or with very unimpressive research records, with a resultant probable decline in the quantity and quality of academic research. The kind of Gresham's law which operates in this field to permit immediate, often routine, duties to drive out long-term, costly, and often tedious research, will find a fillip in the pressures which large enrollments and teacher shortages will soon produce.

[32] See *Teachers for Tomorrow* (New York: Fund for the Advancement of Education, 1955), especially pp. 60–62. See also *Manpower and Education*.

2. Characteristics of the Administrative Setting for Research

For forms of government, let fools contest;
Whate'er is best administer'd is best.

Alexander Pope, *Essay on Man*

AS NOTED in the first part of chapter 1, there are very different basic attitudes and approaches among academicians toward the role of research, especially in the colleges. Even where there is an emphasis upon the importance of research, for its own values and for what it contributes to more invigorated teaching and the prestige of the institution, there are attitudes often not greatly dissimilar from those which constrain the researcher in institutions where research is not strongly encouraged. In interviews with academic personnel—from graduate teaching assistants up through the ranks of full professors, deans, and presidents—one hears the same observations over and over about the conditions, or the setting, for research.[1]

These same kinds of comments have been reported in some of the Carnegie Endowment self-survey reports and in other reports and studies bearing on the subject of academic research. There are exceptions to the following conditions for those persons who work in large research centers on university campuses, but they are the exception and not the pattern for research at most academic institutions.

---

[1] The conditions, or the setting, for research in international relations do not differ markedly from those pertaining to other fields of research, especially in the social sciences. The fact that they are not unique did not seem an argument for not reporting them here.

Tendency of Researchers To Work Alone

The most common condition for research in international relations is that scholars generally work alone. In most institutions only a few people will have a deep interest in international affairs, and only a very few of these persons will develop a subject for research. There seems to be a strong individualistic strain in many college teachers also, and even where there are other persons on the campus doing research in international affairs, each scholar tends to work by himself in his own office or in the library stacks. He works alone and often very quietly on the things that are of particular interest to him. This condition prevails for several possible reasons.

First of all, the researcher often works alone because there is rarely anyone else at his institution who is interested in the precise subject that he finds vital and challenging. His research-mates, so to speak, are often far away. It is much more common to find scholars doing research on the threat of international communism in France, for example, in closer touch (by correspondence and by visits) with colleagues at other and often remote institutions than with colleagues of their own institutions, whose interests may be in some quite different aspect of international affairs—if, indeed, they have any interest in research at all. More extreme cases of this characteristic are to be found, of course, where a researcher's interests are in biographical studies, in area studies of some out-of-the-way part of the world, or in some new or theoretical approach to the nature of international relations.

Working alone is often explained also by the fact of differing teaching schedules, and schedules for other requirements, which sometimes leave colleagues relatively little time for joint research, much less to mull over jointly their respective research work. As noted before, many college teachers teach fifteen or sixteen hours a week with large classes, do seemingly endless administrative chores, nurse extracurricular activities along, and try to make a few extra and sorely needed dollars by giving outside lectures or teaching extension courses. Research suffers in these cases, or else the teacher slows down the pace and quality of his academic work. He often succumbs to these conditions and regards research as something to be read in the journals and not to be done by him in his office or library workroom. The working conditions for teaching and research are usually better in universities than in colleges, but then there may be the offsetting factor of physical dispersion over a large or sprawling campus. The people who have basically common interests in international affairs are too likely to be connected with different departments located in different buildings and also teaching on different schedules.

Inadequate office space, or other working space for research, often forces would-be researchers to find an out-of-the-way corner in the library, or to work in a study at home, and in either case his tendency to isolation is thereby compounded. Not many colleges have adequate faculty rooms for the "bull sessions" which can be very helpful in research work. The institutions which have good research and faculty social center facilities, and make them attractive for use, are providing a lubricant for interdisciplinary thought and discussion which is beyond evaluation but is almost inevitably stimulating for its users. More imagination in arranging, and a little more administrative support in providing, the physical facilities for faculty members to do research and to get together informally to discuss research would pay good dividends at many institutions. The facilities alone will not, of course, produce their use; but if other incentives are present, then the facilities are valuable.

Another explanation which helps account for the characteristic of some researchers' working alone and in quiet is the academician's tendency sometimes to be secretive about his research. Over and over again one encounters this attitude on the part of the researcher who believes he has a revolutionary idea or a novel approach to an old problem, and he is determined that no one shall know of it in detail until it bursts upon the world in published form. The aspiration to be the first to expose some established doctrine or concept, or to drop a blockbuster, debunking bomb on some long-cherished interpretation of some assembled facts about a past event or policy decision, appears to titillate some scholars as they go about their research. The secretive researcher is also spared embarrassment before his colleagues if for one reason or another he never completes his research or is unable to find a publisher for it.

It has been unhealthy for research in general to have such attitudes of secrecy persist. It is encouraging that some of this is breaking down as a consequence of the frequent need to describe research plans in order to obtain outside financial support and of the increased tendency of the foundations to report what their grantees are investigating. At the predoctoral level of research this condition of secrecy does not exist because candidates for degrees must avoid duplicating what others have done, and there is extensive publicity on doctoral dissertation topics. Government research contracts, however, which often require security clearances for the researchers and security classifications on the research projects and the findings, have aggravated this old tendency for cloistered, secretive research.

One more reason for researchers' working alone is that very few institutions apparently have the resources to pay for research assistants for their senior personnel. Graders for examinations and other course exercises and sometimes section discussion leaders may be called upon to do bits of research for professors. This is not much help in most cases, however, to either the professor or the graduate assistant. Often all that the latter has time to do is a sort of mopping-up type of research: checking footnotes, making bibliographies, and preparing an index. The real satisfactions from research are not found in these chores, and so the young assistant gets a dreary picture of research and the professor has no substantive help on the really important parts of his research project. In the mid-depression years the WPA and NYA projects often provided funds which made possible some genuine research work for graduate students. The postwar GI assistance grants, however, called for no work by the students, unfortunately for them and for their professors, and now we seem to be moving into an era of large fellowship grants for graduate students with no work requirements and a student expectation that they have only their own immediate studies to think about. The professors often have little association in joint research projects with these superior students.

In institutions where high-level graduate seminars have been developed and sustained, students may carry on research projects directly related to, or actually a part of, a professor's research program. In some cases this practice may be abused and the professor may become little more than a foreman and editor for a project which in published form carries only his name and makes no reference—or only passing reference—to the persons who did the actual work. On the other hand, it can be argued that if the professor is rigorous in his standards of research work and his timetable for work performance, then this is first-rate training for the student regardless of what becomes of the end product. Graduate students who are exposed to this kind of apparent exploitation will find few surprises in working in government agencies or in other large research projects where almost no one signs what he writes or writes what he signs and where the credit, if any—as well as occasional abuse—goes to persons at higher levels in the hierarchy.

How can the isolation of the researcher be ameliorated? How can his practice of working "in quiet" be modified? Are the changes implied by these two questions based on valid assumptions as prerequisites to better research in international affairs? Are there developments which might flow from such possible changes which would have undesirable consequences for research as well as possibly beneficial effects? These are questions which the author has raised in interviews, and invariably there has been a lively response.

In general the answers to the first two questions involve "more time" and "more money," and the answers to the second two questions have generally been a qualified "yes, but. . . ." type of response.

Working alone may be the best way to preserve a quality of inspiration and a sense of direction which might be lost if exposed to too much joint endeavor. Also, a group can be as narrow in its focus or emphasis as an individual working alone may be. A group may develop "inbreeding," but this is less likely to happen if the membership of the group changes and it is exposed to visiting scholars for occasional projects or seminars.

How Can the Researcher's Isolation Be Ameliorated?

Isolation can be broken down most effectively, it would appear, if researchers are enabled frequently to leave their classrooms and their residences and go to the persons and places where they can meet colleagues and obtain encouragement and assistance through access to relevant materials and through consultations and criticism with others working on comparable projects. Such travel requires leave from classes and other duties and money for the expenses of travel and subsistence and in some cases for other professional expenses.

The leave part of the problem was acute during the early postwar years when enrollments were high and teachers were under heavy pressure to stay on their campuses. In the last few years leaves of absence have not been so difficult to arrange because of lighter enrollments, and when a professor could afford to take leave without pay, his request was usually granted enthusiastically by administrators hard-pressed to meet each monthly payroll. Now teachers are rapidly moving back into the 1946–50 conditions and there will be much more difficulty in obtaining leaves in the years ahead—unless some novel changes are made in teaching practices.

If the concept of a "proprietary" course ("*my* course," "*his* course") could be modified by a concept of instruction in a core of courses by a pool of manpower, each man in the pool being called upon at different times in different courses for what he can do best or better than anyone else on the staff, then the temporary departure of one man could be more easily arranged than if *his* course had to be dropped or taken over temporarily by somebody unfamiliar with it. In fact, the scheduling of teaching assignments might be so arranged that a free week now and then would be no problem and longer periods could be managed. High-speed travel makes possible a fuller use of free time than has ever been possible before, and short leaves of absence can be very fruitful if well planned in advance.

Likewise, the *careful* use of television for large introductory lecture courses could not only bring many students a much better lecturer than they would otherwise have but would also free some of the time of the teacher whose forte is not on the lecture platform but in small discussion groups or in guiding and doing research. Since lecturing is probably the poorest way in which to impart information, there ought to be no great hesitation in boldly experimenting with ways of using fewer and more able lecturers to reach more and more students and letting the other less able lecturers do what they can do well, including directing research seminars and individual study programs.

Another way to release short periods of time for solitary research or for meetings with other researchers would be to modify drastically our pattern of class schedules. Three or five fifty-minute sessions a week simply chop up the week for the teacher and fragment the learning process for the student. Teaching arranged on this pattern, especially lecturing, probably fails to be effective teaching for mature students and in the process handicaps research work. Another much-needed change in schedules is in the direction of trimesters rather than semesters, with the resulting longer school year that will permit students earlier completion of their academic work. Professors might benefit from this change by a schedule requiring them individually to teach only two out of three trimesters yearly if they have substantial research projects justifying concentrated attention.

More time for research could be found if there were bolder management of schedules and manpower resources in our institutions of higher learning. There is good reason to believe also that money could be saved, without loss of quality in teaching and research, especially if colleges and universities set about finding ways to utilize more fully their manpower and plant and equipment.[2]

The truth is that colleges and universities, by being in essence congeries of teachers of highly individualistic characteristics, often use most inefficiently their human resources and the buildings which have been acquired over the years out of spasmodic philanthropy, fitful planning, and unpredictable income and appropriations. The business of higher education is often poorly managed. To bring it to high efficiency would certainly call for some drastic changes in the lives of teachers and students, which no doubt would bring down the wrath of the guardians of what was, the sentimental alumni, and all persons who believe in the superiority of what is familiar as compared with what might be developed if some tough business management were applied to the hallowed, ivy-mantled halls.

More money is the chief need in the eyes of most academic personnel wanting to do more or better research.[3] The cry by researchers for "more money" often is not for salaries for themselves (urgent and justifiable though that would be), except where it would help relieve them of the necessity to do outside chores for extra pay or to teach summer sessions instead of doing research. It is the facilitation of research which primarily concerns a great many scholars. Quite obviously teachers do not choose their profession for the money they will likely make.

[2] Compare *Higher Education in a Decade of Decision,* Report of the Educational Policies Commission (Washington: The Commission, 1957), p. 132.

[3] See the report of the Committee on Research and Creative Activity of the Southern University Conference in 1953 (Vice-Chancellor Edward McCrady of University of the South, chairman of the committee): ". . . all the other causes of the smaller output of research from Southern colleges . . . revolve around a simple and obvious first cause—lack of money."

There is abundant data to show the low-income status of this profession.[4] College teachers choose this profession for other reasons, and even though some teachers do succeed in becoming reasonably affluent, it is usually from their writing, especially textbooks, and not from their teaching that they harvest the bigger incomes. The pursuit of knowledge and the satisfactions in communicating knowledge to young, eager, and hopeful students are also rewards that most teachers find partially compensatory for their lower dollar income. It is really not so surprising, then, that they earnestly seek financial aid for their pursuit of knowledge.

More money is needed for teachers to be able to take leave without pay when their institutions cannot afford even part of their salaries if they go on leave. Sabbaticals are something generally misunderstood in the public mind and vastly overrated for their beneficence. They do not exist at a great many institutions, and they are very inadequate in all but a few places, with a wide range of qualifications and limitations on when and how often they may be taken; for what purposes; at what pay; and with what degree of support for items like contributions to retirement funds, insurance, health benefits, and so on. College administrations and teachers have welcomed programs like the faculty fellowships of the Fund for the Advancement of Education,[5] the Social Science Research Council Faculty research fellowships,[6] and the government awards for research or lecturing overseas. More such programs might make possible many additional leaves of absence for research work in the next few years.

Money is needed increasingly for scholars to travel to pro-

[4] See Beardsley Ruml and S. G. Tickton, *Teaching Salaries Then and Now* (New York: Fund for the Advancement of Education, 1955).

[5] These pay full salary for a year and usually provide other funds for necessary travel in the United States.

[6] These fellowships provide half of a young teacher's salary provided his administration pays the other half of his salary and reduces his normal teaching load by one-half for a period of three years. By July 1955 the Carnegie Corporation had put $930,000 into this splendid research fellowship program. See *Quarterly Report*, Carnegie Corporation of New York, July 1955, p. 3.

fessional meetings; for small conferences with colleagues for a few days to a few weeks; and most commonly, to work with resources not available at their own institutions. The use of "increasingly" above should be emphasized, because the cost of travel has gone up sharply in recent years; yet the funds for travel expenses have actually been reduced, or in some places cut off altogether, where college revenues have gone down sharply. In many cases where full travel expenses formerly were paid for a scholar to participate in the program of a professional meeting, allowances have now been cut to transportation expenses only. In other cases departments have been allowed transportation funds sufficient for only one member of the department to attend a professional meeting each year, regardless of whether more than one from the department is on the program. Car pools can sometimes manage to overcome this limitation, but not when professional association meetings are two or three thousand miles distant. In some states the teachers of state-supported schools receive no travel expenses for trips beyond the borders of the state; this obviously is not helpful if the scholar lives on one coast and his professional meetings are on the other coast. In privately supported colleges and universities, including some of the most eminent, the allowances for travel expenses for professional meetings are limited, nonexistent, or highly unpredictable from year to year.

Travel expenses for consultations with colleagues or for individual research work are usually even more difficult to obtain than are funds for a faculty member to participate in a large professional meeting since the institution may rightly expect some measure of useful publicity from his appearance on the program. In some institutions small research funds may be drawn on for travel to do research, provided it can be established that the materials to be studied cannot otherwise be reviewed (say, by microfilm, or interlibrary loan, or by having the materials copied at the site), and provided also that the cost is not large. Often the scholar is expected to pay part of the cost of such travel himself. In rare cases the travel fund is a revolving fund, and reimbursement is expected whenever, and however, the borrower can arrange it.

Almost all scholars interviewed lamented most of all this lack of travel money. Without some financial help they are hobbled to their home institutions, cut off from satisfactory communication with their colleagues, and deprived of working where there are the best materials, including their big "laboratory": the world —centers of government, industrial and agricultural power, and cultural wellsprings. Perhaps scholars should take a leaf out of the businessman's book and fight for tax relief on "necessary expenses for research" on a broader base than is now permitted under "professional expenses."

The Social Science Research Council has operated since 1926 a program of grants-in-aid for researchers in the social sciences who do not have access to adequate funds for research including travel funds. This program has been supported by the Rockefeller Foundation, and it has been of inestimable value in making possible good research which otherwise might never have been done, nor done so well. For six years (1948–53) the Social Science Research Council also managed a program of travel grants for area research (along with a program of area research training fellowships), which made possible travel to foreign countries and also travel in the United States for many who might not have had such good opportunities to get to their "laboratories."[7] The Guggenheim Foundation fellowships and other foundation programs have also been helpful to many scholars in supplementing other research grants or by themselves making possible research which would otherwise have been beyond the scholars' means.

As noted earlier, there are various programs for overseas study, but many of them require longer leaves of absence than can be

[7] The council awarded about $700,000 which enabled 214 individuals to carry on research in virtually every accessible part of the world. See *SSRC Items* VII (December 1953), 37–42, for a very interesting review of this excellent program.

obtained. For a scholar who has a special need to use foreign materials or consult with foreign colleagues the summer study tours abroad[8] sometimes offer opportunities. Enterprising scholars can "work their way" across the ocean and then have some time free for their own research.

Money is needed not only for outgoing travel but also to make possible a teacher's bringing in an outside scholar for a seminar, for example, or for a faculty-student forum on some research problem of general interest. If more of this consulting could be done on research methodology as well as on actual research undertakings (or possible research topics), there would be much benefit to students and to teachers.

There are also possibilities for encouraging research in more elaborate conference series by bringing in a number of scholars for several days. The Brookings Institution Seminars on American Foreign Policy were helpful in this respect, as have been the Harris Memorial Foundation Lectures at the University of Chicago, and in recent years the series of lecture conferences (on Southeast Asia, Africa, etc.) by the School of Advanced International Studies of the Johns Hopkins University, from which have resulted useful books as well as a considerable stimulus to research in the papers read and in the discussion of the papers. Another pattern of this kind has been that of the Institute of Politics at Williams College and the Institute of Public Affairs of the University of Virginia, both of which have been suspended. These latter conclaves however, tended more toward adult education than to the stimulation of research, but they did bring some scholars together in circumstances that were helpful to research work.

[8] Consult for example the programs of the American College Council for Summer Study (Newton, Mass.); the Council on Student Travel (New York); the Experiment in International Living (Putney, Vt.); the National Education Association, Division of Travel Service (Washington, D.C.); the United States National Student Association, Educational Travel, Inc. (New York); etc. The Social Science Research Council announced in late summer of 1957 a program of travel grants for scholars residing in the United States to attend selected international congresses and conferences during the next three years.

Assistance Needed by the Individual Scholar

It was mentioned earlier that funds are needed by many scholars for research assistants. Some institutional research resources provide for funds of this kind on a small scale, but it is more often provided for clerical assistance (typing, editing, and filing) than for genuine research help. Perhaps as enrollments increase, the revenues of colleges and universities may increase to the point where research assistants can be provided for scholars in addition to the teaching assistants who will be needed to help carry the burden of large classes. But larger enrollments also will put other demands on the increased tuition revenues.

Research-minded business corporations might consider favorably this potentially effective means of increasing the amount of research in international affairs (and in other subjects) as well as of providing earned income at "learning" jobs for young graduate students.

The purchase of materials often poses another form of financial need for a researcher in the field of international affairs. Foreign books and foreign periodicals and newspapers are scarce items in many college libraries and are particularly hard to come by either on a current delivery basis or in full sets of back issues. Microfilm copies of some material may be had—at reasonable cost— but it is still an item of expense for which many researchers do not have the financial means. Even if researchers can get the microfilm, there often is the problem of a reading machine or other reproduction devices, articles which again are frequently lacking in college libraries. Even buying all the American materials that a scholar thinks he needs may prove beyond the resources of the modest library or departmental book and periodical purchasing funds of the average college and for many universities.[9]

---

[9] In 1954 the American Political Science Association encouraged the establishment of a book rental service for social scientists whose libraries did not have and perhaps could not afford the new books they needed. Robert Oshins was the originator of this idea, and the author, then executive director of the APSA, urged its utility on APSA members.

The purchase of materials is sometimes only a part of the cost of making them usable for research workers and especially for seminars or classes. Binding of pamphlets, periodicals, and paperbound books is essential to safeguard the material. Careful cataloguing and indexing may be called for where there is a quantity of elusive material, and then space and maintenance care must be provided to keep them usable. All these costs, and sometimes others, are involved in the acquisition of research materials, and unfortunately the servicing of materials has become more and more costly (despite the usual low pay in academic libraries), just as the cost of the materials has also increased in most cases.

The researcher is in another "squeeze" on materials as well as on travel: at the very time when there is more and more needed to be bought at higher and higher costs, he has had generally fewer and fewer dollars to work with from his own institution. Library budgets, like travel budgets, have no "tenure" for protection, and they are often among the first to be cut in budget reductions. Pooling of library resources, dividing up areas of subject materials to be purchased, and an expansion of interlibrary loan and copying devices have helped somewhat to meet the need, but they have not been altogether satisfactory measures.

There are many problems in the acquisition and fruitful use of library holdings in the field of international affairs. For example, the quantity of material recently published has raised questions of how to control and plan library holdings. There has been a great outpouring of United States Government documents and United Nations documents, to say nothing of the publications of other governmental bodies in the international field, which are a veritable flood by themselves. To handle even a part of this material adequately is very time-consuming for library staffs and hence expensive. If libraries, in addition, are asked to build up helter-skelter collections of all kinds in a wide variety of subjects in international affairs, there will inevitably be considerable duplication of incomplete collections, at great cost, in many parts of the country.

A more logical system, and one which ideally ought to be adopted, would be for each institution and its library to settle on some single area or a major country or some aspect of international relations, and then buy or accept gifts and exchanges only for that particular specialization. These acquisitions would, of course, be in addition to the very general and basic reference works and periodicals for standard courses in international affairs. On its face this system seems to have much merit. There are considerations, however, which make it not only unlikely of realization but undesirable even if it were otherwise feasible.

There is no denying the immense amount of materials which year after year remain unused in most libraries of colleges and universities. It is also true that much of this material is to be found in other (sometimes nearby) library collections. However, a relevant question is: How did this condition come about? It came about, usually, by virtue of the "orders" of teachers on the faculty pursuing their research interests and endeavoring to meet the requirements in library materials for their students and courses. The interests of scholars often change quite radically, and as a consequence early research collections may be left practically unused while new collections are being built up. Furthermore, there is a high degree of mobility in academic life, especially on the part of young, active, and vigorous research scholars, who move from one institution to another in order to obtain promotions in rank, better pay, better research facilities, and the like. When they leave, the library collections they had started may be left, subsequently unsupported and unused. At the new institution the scholar begins again to build or develop the research resources which will serve his research interests and teaching needs, always, of course, within the limitation of regular library budgets and the possibilities of gifts of materials and funds to the library. This description could be enlarged upon, but most academicians will recognize it as a familiar story. It is not ideally logical, efficient, or desirable, but it does exist, and unless some very basic changes are made, it will continue with only minor modifications.

To change this system would require a degree of authoritarian control over library acquisitions which is utterly unthinkable in our system of higher education, or would require a measure of self-control by scholars and libraries which is extremely improbable. Libraries are on college campuses to serve the needs of students, faculty, and such additional users as the library may choose or be required by law (if it is a state institution) to serve. But the ordering of books—that is, the determination of what is to be in the library—is very largely a function reserved to the institution's faculty.

If college faculties continue to have the primary responsibility for library acquisitions, there will be virtually no way to control in any "ideal" form the collections libraries build up with a view to having one library eventually have the *only* adequate collection on, say, Venezuela or atomic energy for peaceful international economic development, while all other libraries have their single, complete, specialized collections in international affairs in addition to what they must have for general teaching purposes. One of the satisfactions, or perhaps compensations, a low-paid college professor enjoys and defends stoutly is his freedom to venture into fields of learning which he has not previously explored, to offer courses on such subjects, and to modify or abandon his research or teaching of them at a later time when his interests or other circumstances or conditions suggest or urge further changes.

The sad fact remains, it would appear, that the academic library will unavoidably be inefficient in terms of the holdings it acquires and the use made of them by resident faculty which, as it changes its composition and research interests, tends to neglect or completely disregard materials once actively in use. Who can say when these materials may be used again? Not the librarian, certainly, nor even the deans and president. The officers who do the hiring of faculty and research assistants may try, for example, to hire a Latin-Americanist (if one is needed) who will be interested in research on Brazil because their college has a fine library collection on Brazil, only to discover that they cannot get such a man in the rank and pay range they are then able to offer. But even if they do get one who seems to fill the bill, the new recruit may later change *his* interests to problems of inter-American cooperation or some altogether different subject for which the Brazilian collection probably will be of little use.

There is probably no satisfactory answer to this admitted dilemma of constantly burgeoning library collections, with erratic, spasmodic, and sometimes insignificant use of the materials held and serviced at ever-increasing cost.[10] Efforts to specialize in building library collections have not been very rewarding to either scholars or librarians, and they may, in fact, simply compound the possibility of there being, at one time or another, incomplete use of some very extensive library collections. Inter-library loan arrangements, microfilm, and other devices may help a little, but the real solution probably lies in more time free for travel for scholars to do peripatetic research, and the money to make this travel and "visiting" study possible.

Administrative Setting in Large Research Centers

Questions were raised earlier in this chapter regarding the possibility of ameliorating the isolation in which a great many researchers in international affairs are obliged to do their work and the possibilities also of modifying the fairly common tendency of researchers to work in quiet. There may be good answers to these questions and there also may be offsetting disadvantages consequent to such efforts. Conditions of longstanding and widespread prevalence are not easily overcome. The concept of an integrated, well-staffed, and reasonably self-sufficient research center based at some major university offers one possible solution to these questions.

---

10 One thoughtful research worker proposed the idea of a foundation-supported "bank" for unused special collections which have been left behind at some institutions by our modern wandering scholars. The bank would receive an institution's unwanted materials and see that they got to some center or centers where they would be used. Donors to the bank could also draw on it for materials they wanted in a kind of exchange or clearinghouse operation.

Isolation of the researchers obviously is substantially diminished if a large number of scholars interested in Russian studies, or in problems of elites, or in pressure groups in foreign affairs, to use a few examples, are brought together in one academic center. Instead of being scattered across the country from Seattle to Boston, they will be in adjoining offices or study cubicles and can easily—will, in fact, almost perforce be obliged to—consult with each other. Those other scholars who cannot join the center for one reason or another may at least be able to visit it from time to time, and on leaves of absence take up a temporary residence at or near the research center concerned with their research interests.[11] When the visiting scholars return to their home institutions, they will probably be reinvigorated with new ideas and stimulated by association with a group of like-interest scholars. The big research centers now serve a useful general professional purpose, besides their own research, in giving this kind of stimulus to researchers from colleges with little or inadequate research resources for some of their faculty.

The big research center concept runs into difficulties very often, however, in this same area of isolation. In this case the isolation is not so much from other scholars with like research interests but in isolation from graduate students and their beneficial questioning, sparked sometimes by what they are learning in other courses or disciplines wholly outside international affairs. Numerous research workers in some of the best-known international affairs research centers have almost no contact with graduate students on a continuing basis through one or two years, and do not have the experience of joint teacher-and-student planning and wrestling with the writing of an acceptable master's thesis or doctoral dissertation. Isolation of this kind is more costly than some of the researchers in these centers may realize.

There is an observable tendency at some institutions where

[11] Faculty and research fellows under several programs have gone from all over the nation to the big research centers at Harvard, Massachusetts Institute of Technology, Stanford, Princeton, Cornell, Columbia, etc., for just these reasons.

there are large research centers, especially if they are highly specialized centers, for the established regular faculty to look askance at these specialized centers. Since the researchers at the center usually have no teaching or very few teaching duties, usually no administrative duties within the faculty, and none of the chores of university representation which deans and presidents often pass on to their faculties, they are apt to be regarded rather enviously like the lilies of the field who "toil not neither do they spin," but only (somehow) lay up "treasures" in the form of published articles, monographs, and books in quantity, while the overburdened teacher struggles for years to get an item or two of research ready for publication.

Sometimes this tension over different work loads is abetted by the belief, not always accurate, that the people in the research centers are better paid and have more funds for travel and purchase of materials than the regular faculty. The researchers in turn often resent their lack of tenure and academic rank. If the research projects of the center are being done for, or with, United States government agencies and there are security restraints upon publishing or even discussing the research in progress, then the researcher at the center is pushed farther into isolation, away from the outside community of scholars and is made more suspect in the eyes of some of his regular academic neighbors. In these circumstances the relations between regular faculty and center research personnel may range from fair to very poor, and it is a rare place where they could be called excellent. Administrators of research centers should be very wary that just because their working conditions may be more healthy and their research resources and facilities more wealthy, they are not necessarily more wise than the scholars outside the research center.

It is quite evident that the big or sizable research center does have many advantages accruing from a group of scholars working together with few, if any, distractions or diversions from their research. They can protect each other from one of the factors which often inhibits men from publishing research which they have done alone—namely, the fear of the fatal flaw, one or two crucial little points they have completely overlooked which would have been caught by a closely associated research colleague. It is also clear that many of the research centers do have far more money for travel, for the purchase of materials, for clerical and research assistance, for office space, and for the costs of publication and distribution of their research findings than the average individually self-supported scholar. Identification with a well-known research center may also be helpful to the researcher who sets forth to do field research, including interviews, or in obtaining access to classified government materials. Wherever possible research centers ought to make special efforts to include in their programs, and share their advantages with, the regular faculty of their institution and perhaps of neighboring institutions also. A little more attention to the politics of good human relations would have paid huge dividends in closer cooperation, better morale, and *better research* at some of these specialized research centers.

The research centers in many cases have been very effective in breaking down the tendency of scholars to work in quiet. As a general practice they receive outside financial aid only after they have spelled out in considerable detail the subjects they propose to research, the publications they envisage from their research, the time, staff, and money needed for the research, and so on. It seems to be increasingly common practice for the philanthropic foundations (to whom such requests are usually addressed) to ask outside scholars to review the prospectuses of such proposed projects or to subject them to the review of committees of scholars established for such purposes or regularly established (like some of the committees of the Social Science Research Council or of the professional learned associations). Many people, by this means, will know well in advance of any grant what so-and-so or such-and-such institution is proposing for a research project. This is exactly the opposite of the traditional practice of each scholar keeping his research secret to himself. Research centers also frequently publish brochures announcing their projected research (usually after they have received financing), or members of the staff read papers at professional meetings or write articles or research notes for the appropriate professional journals.[12]

Quarterly reports and annual reports of some of the major foundations give fairly detailed information on the research plans of research centers or groups they have financed, and these, like the reports of the Social Science Research Council, the American Council of Learned Societies, and the journals of the professional associations, reach many thousands of readers.[13] The *quid pro quo* for financial support for research from nonacademic as well as from normal academic sources is increasingly that of publicity or information about research plans, publications out or in prospect, and the personnel working on research projects. This is a healthy and long overdue development. Even the ill-advised and badly managed congressional inquiries into the activities of tax-exempt foundations may have helped serve this objective of more information about who is doing what research at which locations, on what basis of support, and with what expectations and plans for publication.[14]

[12] See, for example, the brochure of the Center for the Study of American Foreign Policy at the University of Chicago; the article by Clyde Kluckhohn in *World Politics,* I (January 1949), 267–72, on "Russian Research at Harvard"; the reports of the Russian Institute of Columbia University; the brochure of the Foreign Policy Analyses Project of the Organizational Behavior Section of Princeton University; the brochure of the Massachusetts Institute of Technology Center for International Studies, "The Center for International Studies: A Description," July 1955.

[13] Publicity is sometimes given to large research programs in newspapers such as the *New York Herald Tribune* and the *New York Times.*

[14] If this was a considerable achievement, it came about inadvertently insofar as the investigators were concerned. Some of the best information on social science research is to be found in the lengthy replies of some of the foundations and research councils to the accusations and innuendos of the staff of the Special Committee of the House of Representatives To Investigate Tax-Exempt Foundations and some of the members of the investigating committee themselves. Happily, it is an ill wind that blows no good. The little gem on social science research by Pendleton Herring of the Social Science Research Council (the only rebuttal the Reece Committee permitted to be made in public hearings) is almost worth all the grief and wasted time and money of that ill-starred investigation. See *Annual Report* of the SSRC, 1953–54, pp. 20–34; also see the report of the Committee.

One of the by-products of would-be researchers' being required to outline rather fully a proposed project is the improvement and increased appreciation of project designing. More and more it has become clear that a poorly planned research project will almost certainly result in poorly performed and inadequate research. The investment of even a little money to study the feasibility, desirability, and necessary conditions for a given research proposal have paid off very well in end results.[15]

As researchers in international affairs recognize more fully the contributions possible from disciplines previously not much consulted in such research (for example, psychology, anthropology, and sociology), there is a greater need to *plan* research projects carefully and cooperatively regardless of how they may later be carried out. In this endeavor the individual researcher in international affairs is not likely to be so well situated as the member of a research center where careful planning and periodic review of research plans is a normal operating procedure. The individual researcher, however, can make use of the advice of colleagues at his own or other institutions, or sometimes he can try out his plan of research at a professional meeting. Faculty seminars may also be a possible medium for joint planning as well as discussion of research projects. These developments are all to the good, for even if there is an initial slowing-down of research output, it may mean that fewer researchers will plunge into a great forest of problems ill-equipped to do what they have hastily undertaken.

Administrative or Organizational Aids to Research

There has been a growing realization in the academic institutions of the need to have some better administrative organization to foster research in the social sciences, including work in international affairs. In a number of institutions there are councils or institutes for social science research, and they vary from being well organized, well managed, and quite helpful and effective to

[15] The experience of the American Political Science Association and its affiliate, the Governmental Affairs Institute, in previewing carefully and critically proposed research projects is a good illustration of the values to be derived from this practice.

being little more than "paper" organizations of no real value. Besides such institutes there are other possibilities in administrative organization and services, which are just beginning to be explored and developed, comparable to some of the highly developed administrative devices for research in the natural sciences.

The University of North Carolina has had an Institute for Research in the Social Sciences since 1924, which is the same year in which the Social Science Research Council was organized, and it is perhaps the oldest such university research agency in the United States. Howard W. Odum was the founder of the institute and its director for the first twenty years. He developed the program of the institute, which in many ways has been a model for such enterprises. The objectives of the institute have been to encourage and stimulate research in the social sciences at the University of North Carolina, to design and plan for coordinated research programs, to find and develop research personnel, to be a training center for research personnel in collaboration with the established social science departments of the Graduate School of the university, and to serve as a facilitating center for cooperation with other agencies for developing procedures for making research (especially in a regional framework) of more functional value.[16]

While this institute has done little directly in the field of international affairs, it has performed an extraordinarily useful service in stimulating research in the social sciences and in helping train personnel who either have already turned, or may later turn, their talents to research in international affairs. Other institutions seeking a pattern for the development of an *organizational* entity and a set of *general objectives* would do well to study the experience of over thirty years of this institute.

Judging from some of the institutional self-surveys in the Carnegie Endowment project, some institutions are studying ways of

[16] Gordon W. Blackwell, *Annual Report of the Director, 1953–54*, Institute for Research in Social Science, University of North Carolina (Mimeographed: Chapel Hill).

giving better *administrative support* in their institutions to research in international affairs, either as a specific body of research activity or as a part of the much larger area of research in the social sciences in cooperation with other cognate disciplines. A broadly representative committee of social scientists at the University of Texas[17] has been making such a study in a very thorough manner. This committee has studied the administrative arrangements at several institutions for encouraging and supporting social science research with particular attention to several aspects of administrative organization and action. These aspects include: (a) the degree to which channels of communication regarding, and support for, research are centralized in one organization on the academic campus; (b) the amount of control and authority invested in the research organization; (c) the amount of autonomy of the organization; (d) the rate of expenditure per annum for social science research; (e) the amount of external support (foundation, government, individual endowment) received by the academic institution for the development of social science research; (f) amounts of internal support (administrative and faculty) for social science research (for such matters as faculty research leaves of absence, departmental research assistants, clerical and technical aid, publication of research, travel allowance to scientific meetings, and related general aids to research); and (g) other matters such as the degree to which interdisciplinary research is characteristic of the research organization, and the tradition and conditions pertaining to research before any formal research organization was attempted or established. Merely to enumerate the range of problems pertinent to the question of how to organize and operate programs for social science research at an academic institution is enough to suggest the complexity and inherent difficulty in this kind of undertaking.

This report will not deal with all these administrative aspects and problems, but it is worth noting that more and more institu-

[17] Committee on Research in the Social Sciences, Dr. Robert L. Sutherland, director, the Hogg Foundation, University of Texas, chairman.

tions concerned about their contributions to research in international affairs are giving careful study to the administrative need for organizing and supporting such research. In interviewing research scholars and administrative officers at numerous institutions, the author encountered a wide range of opinion with respect to these administrative developments or possibilities, and the effect which they might have on research work. There was much concern about the pros and cons of research institutes in an institution and also concern about cooperative institutes with several institutions participating.[18]

The most controversial question in this whole complex of administrative support is probably centered around the matter of the amount of authority and control which any administrative organization should have over academic research activity. On the one hand there is considerable evidence that a vigorous academic administrative organization for research can attract more financial support for research than can individual scholars left to their own devices. If presented in the name of the institution rather than in the name of an individual or even of a single department or school, a request for research funds may be more favorably considered by a foundation, a private donor, or a government agency. There is more assurance to the prospective donor that the research proposed is considered important if it has been carefully reviewed by impartial, as well as the immediately interested, parties. There is also the prospect that the proposed research will more likely be carried out satisfactorily since the institution has endorsed it and is prepared to support it than if only a small group or a single individual is sponsoring the project. To obtain institutional endorsement for applications for research assistance implies, however, a certain screening process for proposed research projects which may have draw-

[18] The Oak Ridge Institute of Nuclear Studies is an example of a successful and well-regarded cooperative research center with over thirty colleges and universities in the South cooperating to take advantage of research facilities. The M.I.T. Center for International Studies has done something like this in the Cambridge-Boston area.

backs as well as advantages. The prospect of a kind of censorship appears when the element of administrative review of research projects is proposed.[19]

A number of scholars interviewed on this question admitted some advantages in institutional endorsement, but they also seemed to fear a possible undesirable extension of administrative review and control of proposed research as a precondition to institutional endorsement of application for foundation grants or government contracts. If an institution directs its faculty not to make direct approaches to foundations or government agencies, but to seek funds only through administrative channels—which may or may not endorse the proposed research project—all kinds of possibilities may eventuate from this practice. Admittedly there are good possibilities from such practices, such as more money might be obtained on better terms than if an individual applies (as noted above); institutional resources might be better used for some projects than others; better research might be done; and over a period of years the institution's standing for research work in international affairs might be enhanced by more institutional planning and control, thereby making it easier to obtain subsequent support.

There are possibilities, however, that individual scholars who do not thrive in planned and formal environments will be suffocated in such a system. The research proposals of an individual scholar may not be in accord with the administration's ideas—or even in accord with the ideas of his faculty colleagues—as to what is appropriate for the institution to be identified with. If there is a conservative administrative attitude toward political affairs, there may be no enthusiasm or support for research projects that might bring the institution publicity of a kind which the administration would consider embarrassing.[20] There may

---

[19] Review procedures by foundations and government selection boards also often have suppressing effects, and some potentially good materials may be cut off from aid by conservative or faddist standards of review.

[20] The author knows of one case where a small grant for research was withheld until the applicant before the institutional research council agreed to

be a tendency to try to keep faculty research concentrated on subjects in which the institution already has considerable research resources in order to avoid having to acquire new materials,[21] whereas, as noted earlier, scholars have a penchant for breaking out into new fields of research as a way of satisfying their search for knowledge and expressing their cherished freedom and liberty of action.

Some scholars also see dangers of a kind of pro-rata parceling out of assistance,[22] or a kind of logrolling procedure in the operation of administrative review of research proposals. They note that if the reviewing body is an interdepartmental, interdisciplinary committee, there will be a tendency to overlook the relative merits of individual research projects in order to be sure that every department obtains some support even if some departments have weaker projects than others. If the review is by administrative officers, there is the belief that "politics" may enter into the decision to give or withhold support and that scholars who have been bothersome to the administration will fare less well than the stooges or "milquetoasts" who have never done battle with the administration. While some scholars concede that their fears about administrative review of proposals for research funds may be exaggerated, they often take the position that there is no comparable substitute for the inspired scholar who pursues without restraint his quest for knowledge wherever it may lead him, and that foundations and the government should support such scholars regardless of whether they have the official backing or blessing of their colleagues or the institution's administrative officers.

---

change the title of his research topic so that the institution might not appear to be involved in the study of the controversial subject of the Communist revolution in China.

[21] In this regard it might be said that research grants to individuals sometimes lead to expenditures and commitments by institutions in ways which the individuals did not visualize or anticipate but which would have been foreseen if the project had been given prior administrative review.

[22] This appears to have happened recently at some institutions which received large grants for studies in the behavioral sciences.

Research Contracts for Government Projects

Some universities have been concerned about the extent to which the research centers (of various kinds) that have been created since World War II may be drawing the institutions of higher learning away from their main purposes—the advancement and diffusion of knowledge—for the sake of lucrative government contracts or foundation grants for specific, detailed, and often operational—rather than basic—research.[23] The increase in free and unrestricted research in many fields, including that of international affairs, is not in direct proportion to the increase in funds for research since World War II. It is doubtful, too, that there has been a comparable increase in the number of persons trained for research in international affairs in relation to the increased amount of money provided for big research projects. The increase in the number of postwar doctorates in international affairs, for example, while not reliably measurable, would not seem to be in proportion to the great increase in funds given for research since World War II.[24] However, it is clear that many elements are involved in this question besides the element of financing.

The limiting of research to specific, operational needs of government agencies not only may be stultifying to the development of research per se and mechanical or routine work for the researcher, but it also runs the risk of controverting the essence of academic research, as expressed in the commendable motto of Stanford University—"Let the Winds of Freedom Blow." Free-ranging, open, and even heretical research has been one of the great contributions of universities ever since a concept of organized higher learning took shape. To bring secrecy onto the

[23] President Harold W. Dodds of Princeton, for example, has inveighed against this proclivity for "projectitis."

[24] See the report of the Commission on Organization of the Executive Branch of the Government, on *Intelligence Activities* (Washington: Government Printing Office, 1955), p. 14. This report was notably silent on external research, but, because of the brevity of the report, this need may have been implied more than explicitly described.

campus and invest it with large funds and some of the best of our limited supply of able academic researchers is to challenge the very essence of a university's *raison d'être*.

A genuine dilemma exists in this situation, for, despite the thousands of persons doing research in the so-called federal "intelligence community," in at least some twelve distinct major departments of the government, there apparently is a need by our government for more research and intelligence data from behind the iron curtain—Russia and her satellites and Communist China. If external governmental research is to be developed further, what will be the effect of this kind of activity on the normal teaching and research functions of our institutions of higher learning? In several leading institutions some able and distinguished scholars have more or less "gone underground" to do contract research for the government. While so occupied they can say little about what they are doing. One eminent scholar in the field of American foreign policy complained to the author that he was for some time estopped from even talking about a major research project even after he had finished it for the government. As a further aggravation he sees no evidence of his research having been used, and he is now wary of doing any further writing on the subject of his government research (a subject he knows well, which was why he was chosen to make the study) until he has a release from the government security restraint.

In the long run this kind of suffocation and hobbling of future research could be gravely serious to research in general and to the teaching of new generations of American citizens. This is only one consequence of a "garrison state" type of mentality, but this one is a real menace to research and to researchers. The chief remedy seems to lie in a more relaxed concept of security classifications and a more frequent review for declassification of research which has been classified secret or top secret.

More fundamentally we need a greater emphasis on basic research and on research uninhibited by project limitations of any but the very broadest outlines. If operational research is needed beyond what can be done in the intelligence community of the Federal Government, then it might better be done at centers not connected with institutions of higher learning where it may prove to be more diversionary from the main purpose of such institutions than its possible benefits may be worth. It is essential that a large part—if not all—of the research work of centers of learning be kept free, uncommitted, and responsive to the needs for research on topics which only those who are free and un-hampered by political controls will dare, or be able, to undertake.

As in many matters academic, there is no simple solution to this problem of how best to organize and maintain strong administrative support for research in international affairs, or in any branch of knowledge for that matter. Administrators and supporters are properly concerned about the most efficient use of institutional resources (personnel and other), the over-all prestige of the institution (which can be damaged by ill-considered research applications to outside agencies, carelessly conducted research, or by publication of ill-performed research), and the need to meet other financial demands upon the income and sources of general support for the institution. Scholars are concerned about unrestrained freedom to investigate, to report, and to theorize on their research, and to receive the financial and other administrative support which they think their research projects warrant. Even Solomon might be perplexed by the problem of reconciling these different interests. The answer would seem to lie somewhere between complete *laissez faire* for the scholars, which has not been adequate in many respects, and an overcentralized and bureaucratic authority, which could be stultifying for research in international affairs and which is bound to involve controversial subjects and, hence, frequent bothersome problems for administrators. The ideal would be to offer research services and support on a take-it-or-leave-it basis but made attractive to individual scholars, and yet not put the assistance wholly beyond the control of the administration whose major responsibility is to serve, and preserve, the interests and objectives of all its faculty, students, and the community which keeps the institution operating.

Conclusion

The pros and cons of arguments over administrative conditions and support for research range over a very wide field of opinion. It is probably a truism to say that what works well at one institution may not work well when copied by another institution. Personality factors, the general setting, and the motivation are different. Efforts to organize research centers have gone well at some institutions and other ventures at the same institutions have fared badly. There is, in brief, no certainty of satisfaction in any particular form or organization.

The individual scholar, working mainly alone, will continue, no doubt, to be the chief producer of research in international affairs. Large staffs doing "grouped" research may be more productive where the type of research undertaken calls for cooperative effort and substantial financing. In a few cases interdisciplinary research teams may succeed in realizing fruitful undertakings, but this has not proved to be a very useful device. In all administrative settings there will be a need for money and equipment (including mechanical instruments) in greater quantity than ever before if research in international affairs is to continue to thrive and be more scientific and thorough.

3. Organization and Methods for Research

The Chaos is come of organized disorder,
The consistently inappropriate and the simple wrong.

George Baker, *First American Ode*

THERE has been discussion previously of the most common characteristic of research in international relations at American colleges and universities: namely, that scholars tend to work alone, except at a few large institutions where specialized research centers have developed, especially since World War II. Each teacher preparing for his lectures and his seminars, or guiding and planning the work of graduate students, digs out for himself, almost invariably by himself, what he needs for these purposes. When he goes beyond these tasks or mixes them with the writing of articles, monographs, or even books, he usually does the work predominantly by himself.

Organizational Arrangements for Research

Practices were noted earlier of using graduate students and research assistants for spade work and for odds and ends of research checking, but the bulk of the research done by the vast majority of scholars is essentially a one-man production. Frequently two or more men may collaborate on writing a textbook or a book of readings. Sometimes a team, perhaps a teacher and one of his former graduate students, will cooperate on an article or a monograph, but such enterprises are rare rather than common, as may be seen from a perusal of the tables of contents of learned journals or from bibliographies of books published in this field. Very rarely one encounters joint applications for research grants by a team of two researchers, unless Cupid has had a hand in the team-up and the pair are man and wife. More two-member teams might be effective in joint research work, but even where this is undertaken it is usually a division of labor rather than a down-the-line sharing of research.

A division of labor can be an effective device given clear prior agreement as to what is being divided and how the work is to be done. Once again, if there were more money available for travel to permit frequent consultations by researchers who have the confidence of other colleagues, either in this country or abroad, much more could be done by team research without the administrative paraphernalia and the expense of a big research center.

Strengthening team research might result in more pairs of home institutions benefiting from the probably improved and invigorated research of their staff members, and this in turn would almost certainly be reflected in better teaching and related educational services by these faculty members. Multiply this process several times, and a general uplifting of research in international affairs would ensue at our colleges and universities, including some of those not now noted for the research done on their campuses. A team divided between two or more institutions will encounter some problems in cooperating, and these may be serious unless the participants assign a top-priority position to this joint research.

A further promising form of cooperation is in a team consisting of an academic scholar and a research-minded "operator" working in international affairs. More of this kind of collaboration ought to be developed and assisted by administrators in academic centers and in government.

It might be emphasized here that more research fellowships for periods of several months are not so urgently needed as are the means to go from one's own campus for a few days or a few weeks. A good many fellowship opportunities are not accepted because the length of time they specify is more than is required for some research projects or is longer than is permissible because of the scholar's other duties. A teacher who takes long leaves too often for strictly research purposes may suffer in terms of academic status or salary increases as compared with those who stay close to home base except for short, intensive periods of research at other centers. The best people in any enterprise are often the busiest people: a top researcher-teacher is not infrequently involved in committee work for his institution and in special projects for his professional associations; and in international affairs, he may also be a consultant on call by the government or some international agency or organization. For reasons of these commitments and also because of his probable standard of living and fixed dollar expenses he may not be able to afford to go away for a year on a Fulbright or some other fellowship. But he needs as much as any other scholar frequent opportunity to work with his research colleagues for short periods of consultation and stimulation. This kind of assistance is essential if more team research is to be done.

The Research Center as an Organizational Device

The role of research centers in the study of international affairs has been touched upon previously in relation mainly to the problem of the isolation of scholars. The research center merits discussion also for its contribution to the development of organizational arrangements for research.

By virtue of generous foundation grants to some research centers it has been possible to recruit sizable staffs of researchers for particular projects. Under the guidance of a research director and subdirectors, groups of scholars, often from different disciplines, have undertaken research on fairly sharply defined projects to be completed within stated time intervals. Three operational aspects are worth noting here: (1) the problems of a group working under a manager, (2) concentration on a predetermined topic for research (possibly under a government contract), and (3) a predetermined completion date. Each one of these aspects may be variable: there may be considerable autonomy *within* and *by* the group of researchers with only a minimum of direction from an identifiable director-manager; the research subject may be modified in the course of the work on the project; and delivery dates may be modified for one or more reasons but at some risk to the prestige of the group and of possibly lowered chances for further foundation grants or government contracts, especially if the original delivery dates are very tardily met. There are very considerable differences between this over-all operational pattern of a research center and that of the self-propelled individual scholar, or even a team of two or more scholars, pursuing their research as best they can on whatever timetable they arrange for themselves and manage to fulfill.

Some participants in these group research centers have reported to the author their gratification at being in a center where "things are being done," where there are relatively ample funds and good facilities, and where there is frequent contact with like-minded or like-interest researchers. They have complained, however, of the not infrequent tediousness of group research, such as frequent long conferences for the outlining of objectives, for the assignment of initial tasks, for the review of outlines and then the review of first drafts, and also prolonged discussions over how to phrase conclusions or to reach agreement even on what factual data are, or are not, relevant or important enough to include in a research report. They also complain that since people work at different speeds, in a group project the whole pack-train is held up by the slowest horse on the trail, or by the one who wanders off the main trail to other trails or pastures. They note that in drafting conclusions it is not uncommon for strong statements, which an individual might publish, to be watered down to the lowest level of acceptance by the group or by the director who may have a proper, or an ill-founded, concern for the political repercussions of a given research report unless it is very carefully worded. There is, in brief, a burden of lost motion, friction, too much managing, and too much concern for the politics of the situations in some group research enterprises.

The limitations of a research inquiry to a specific topic with clearly defined limits is often characteristic of the government research contracts frequently undertaken by research centers. Several deficiencies and some dangers are apparent in this practice. Unless there has been careful preliminary exploration and a good design for a major research project, it is presumptuous and probably self-defeating to delimit in advance the range and focus of the study. Without exceptional perception prior to the beginning of research it will be rare indeed that a research project does not perforce extend beyond some of its original outlines and probably fall short in other parts of its outline. There is a grave danger that, if a research center is given too firm and rigid an assignment, the researchers will do little more than fill out a kind of expanded questionnaire from a list of detailed questions or sub-sub-topics of an extensively itemized outline. This has happened in government research contracts and to a lesser degree in some foundation-supported operational-type research work. The consequences of doing such research may seriously affect the motivation and aims of research. One commentator on this problem has noted this possibility and has observed that "what always was considered and done as the highest expression of dedication to truth and to love of a subject of learning has now become frankly a goal-directed activity; yet it is still cloaked in idealistic terms, patriotic and socially approved."[1]

The third aspect noted as characteristic of work at big research centers, whether on government contracts or on foundation grants, is the common requirement that a given research undertaking be completed by a predetermined time. This may be explicit to the extent of an actual delivery date being embodied in a research contract; or it may be implicit in the prospectus submitted to a foundation asking for a grant, and when the grant is made, the date may become frozen, so to speak, by

[1] Mr. M. A. Tuve, in a speech entitled "Technology and National Research Policy," given at the Institute of Public Affairs, University of Virginia, July 9, 1953.

virtue of the time limit put on the grant, or a stated date may be set for completion of one or more stages of a project before additional funds will be supplied. However it may be established, the fact of a fixed or generally accepted terminal date thereafter hangs over the heads of research directors and staff like the proverbial sword of Damocles. This pressure may be good in that it helps offset some of the tendency to overorganize and endlessly debate how to do the research job or how precisely to phrase the research report. It has a real disadvantage, however, in often hastening into completion research findings which are still incompletely thought through. In order to get a contract renewed, a research agency may lower its standards on research quality if this is necessary to deliver a reasonably presentable report. In order to show progress to a foundation or to a government agency, a research center may permit publication of research findings before the research is fully completed or the data are adequately evaluated and tested. In the long run no one really gains from such pressure; there are only regrets over uncreditable research being in circulation.

Time-bound research programs labor under another serious handicap as compared with what might be done by academicians in more normal conditions. When a three- or a five-year research project begins, it may not be too difficult to recruit good research staff, especially if there are ample funds for personnel. As the time limit begins to run out, however, it is often increasingly difficult to hold the best of the research staff, for they are the ones who are usually most eagerly sought after by other research agencies or by institutions for teaching positions. Those who remain are likely to be more and more preoccupied with where they will go next. The research director in this situation faces the double squeeze of time running out and staff running out just at the point where his operation is under the greatest pressure to bring the work to completion with a high level of performance.

Interviews with directors and staffs of research centers attached to some of our universities have revealed some other weaknesses in group research on project programs. A frequently vexing problem is that of assignment of credit in finished research—whose names will go on the title page; who gets credit in the foreword; what magnitude of credit is to be given to different members of the staff, ranging from research director through senior researchers to the research assistants. Who is the final judge of what is acceptable? If the group passes on each researcher's piece of research, how can a log-rolling type of approval be avoided for any and all parts of the job, in order for each person to be certain that his part is approved? These may seem petty questions, but it appears they often affect the morale of researchers.

In the foregoing discussion there may seem to be an overly critical view of group research, especially group research organized in or around research centers. Certainly some of the ills of government contract research on specific subjects apply just as much when the work is done by an individual as when done by a group. Some of the ills of time-bound research grants apply also to individual workers. There is much to be said in favor of the group organization for research, but the point made here is that it is often very costly, often cumbersome, and sometimes not so neat an operational arrangement as it might appear to be. In many cases, it should be noted, the big research centers are not really doing group research in the strict sense of the term, but rather they are doing *grouped* research, with members of the center working quite separately on different aspects of a general focus or central theme. Grouped research is a more feasible and probably a more profitable organizational approach than the earlier concepts of group research, which might or might not be interdisciplinary in the makeup of the staff.

Research Methods Used in International Affairs Research

In recent years there has been a growing concern over methodology[2] in the study of international relations, but it is still a very minor interest of the researchers working in this field. Methodol-

[2] See Daniel Lerner and Harold D. Lasswell (eds.), *The Policy Sciences* (Stanford, Calif.: Stanford University Press, 1951) for a discussion of recent developments in the scope and methods of the social sciences.

ogy per se has not caught the research interest of political scientists so much apparently as it has that of sociologists or historians, and by no means to the same degree as in the natural sciences. The political scientists, and the international affairs specialists particularly, have been preoccupied with writing descriptive and analytical studies of events and problems in their field and have given very little study to the methods used in gathering the data reported or in arriving at the analysis they have presented.[3] In the process of concentrating on descriptive studies in international affairs the researchers in this field appear to have drawn heavily on data gathered by other scholars, notably historians and to a lesser degree economists and sociologists. In the field of research dealing with international organization and international conferences there has been a strong tendency to follow the pattern of research in comparative government, and to concentrate on descriptions of form, structure, and process of institutions. There has been little use of the methods of psychology or anthropology to reveal the reasons for the structure, or to seek the problems imbedded deeply in the conflict of national interests within the organization or conference system.

In reporting research in international affairs it has been rare to find an author discussing in any detail how he arrived at his findings. Most researchers have written their findings on the pattern of Louis Gottschalk's advice: "What the reader wants and is entitled to have is the safe conclusion, the warranted statement, the reasonable belief; he expects the author's mental processes not to show." It might well be argued that there would be genuine benefit to the reader and certainly to other researchers if the authors of research findings in international affairs did let their mental processes and research methods show. There is probably

---

[3] Out of 797 political science research projects studied in 1950, Hawley and Dexter noted that only some 15 at the most could be classified as concerned with methodology, epistemology, or the collection of resource data, Claude E. Hawley and Lewis A. Dexter, "Recent Political Science Research in American Universities," *American Political Science Review*, XLVI (June 1952), 472, 484–85.

not enough reporting in this field of research of the inquiries that have been unproductive and of the inadequacies of certain methods of research (for example, interviewing techniques, questionnaires, opinion polls, and so on) when applied to certain kinds of problems. It would seem that the researchers in the natural sciences and life sciences especially, more often report what did not "pan out," as well as what did "pan out," than do the social scientists. Possibly this difference is explained, as noted earlier, by the preoccupation of research in international affairs in the past years with pure description, with little emphasis on the cause, or the why, or the significance of events, decisions, and attitudes in international affairs. In any case, whether the research went well or poorly, the procedures and processes used by a researcher ought to be observable or discoverable even if the working "scaffolding" of the research projects is removed before the finished product is revealed to public view.

The Study of "The Record": An Approach and a Method

Social scientists, like other scientists, have put much of their effort into collecting facts, the empirical method of research. Like the famous German historian, Ranke, the student of international affairs aspires to "get all the facts" before his conclusions can be ventured safely. Gathering the facts for the study of international affairs has been, and will continue to be, an overwhelming task. The quantity of data purporting to be facts becomes more voluminous each year, and the question of what facts are relevant to the sound study of international affairs also becomes more and more complex and perplexing. The basic attitude toward research in this field undoubtedly remains, however, that of the pre-eminent importance of building up a vast body of verified and incontrovertible facts about the nature and trends of international affairs, past and present. To be reliable knowledge must be based on facts; and to be useful our knowledge ought to provide possibilities for reliable predictions or dependable projections and probabilities.

Given this basic attitude toward the study of international affairs, it is not surprising to find that the vast majority of research going on—and of research done in the postwar years—is a search for the facts, a study of the record of what happened, how it happened, who was responsible or influential in what happened, the recognized alternatives to the decision or action taken at a given time, how international organizations are constructed, function, and grow, and the like. Much of what has been done in the past decade is an analysis of the record plus some reporting from firsthand observation of events or from participation in international conferences, organizations, and other activities involving the conduct of international relations or national affairs bearing on international affairs. The major activity has been in reviewing the record and in analyzing documents in mountainous abundance, without the researcher himself having been a participant in the actions under study. The perusal of bibliographies of research in this field will reveal the extent of this great search for, and presentation of, facts.

Fact-finding as an end in itself is not, however, the whole of research in international affairs despite its apparent predominance. There has been a substantial effort to seek facts for the purpose of supporting limited hypotheses as to national conduct in international affairs; as to the reasons for international organizations taking this, that, or another form; as to why certain decisions were taken and others were not; and similar propositions or speculations. These approaches assume that not all facts are equally relevant, necessary, or even desirable in the study of some particular aspect of international affairs, but that sound research consists of an ordering of those facts which bear directly upon a selected problem or subject of study. The danger in this approach, of course, is that a researcher who has developed a predetermined hypothesis about a given problem will tend to select his facts to fit his hypothesis, and while he reports what is in a sense true and significant, he may not report the whole truth or the full significance. This approach has resulted in partial research in two senses of the word: partial in that it is often fragmentary, and partial in that it is sometimes "slanted" to the researcher's predetermined views of what he hopes to discover and report.

There has been a growing tendency toward developing theories about aspects of international affairs (for example, how a sense of community develops, and the relationship of such a phenomenon to the construction of international organizations) or even theories about the nature of international relations as a whole. Sometimes concepts of an essentially theoretical nature have been expounded with hortatory fervor, which may make them more convincing than they are actually scientific or sound. The grubbing-up of facts and the digging of post-holes in the great field of the unknown bores or does not appeal at all to some researchers, and they prefer to take what facts are readily at hand, venture some interpretations, generalizations, or judgments, announce that they have fenced in a part of the great unknown, and proclaim it for what they believe it to be.

The Problem of Supplementing the Written Record in the Gathering of Facts

While the written record is abundant, in fact overwhelming in many cases, for the researcher in international affairs, there is often a need to supplement the record with more information. If the subject of the research lies in the past so that no personal recollections of it may be obtained, there is not much that a researcher can do except to rely on what has already been recorded. If the subject involves a country not open to an American academic researcher, then the scholar is again forced back upon the record to a very considerable degree. Apart from these qualifications, however, there is normally a wide field of opportunity open to the scholar for supplementing the written record by obtaining additional information from principals, either as individuals or as whole groups of people. Common methods used for supplementing the written record are: (*a*) personal interviews, (*b*) written inquiries and formal questionnaires, (*c*) a combination of both of these methods, and (*d*) participant-observer activities.

This report is not the place for a detailed discussion of these two methods of research in international affairs. Some comments about the utility of these measures to academic researchers are in order, however. The academic researchers seem to have mixed opinions regarding the value of these methods, depending usually on the nature of the subject they are researching, on their physical location (with respect to remoteness from the principals they would like to interview, for example), and the amount of their financial resources to utilize these methods, all which can become quite expensive procedures.

The Personal Interview Method
for Gathering Research Data

The chief advantage of the interview method is that it may draw out hitherto unrecorded information and may also shed new light on what was previously available to the scholar in the written record. Academic researchers are frequently well qualified for interviewing because their profession is a vocal one: as teachers they are accustomed to drawing out students in the discussion of facts and ideas; and, if they have been good researchers in the written records first, they often can go to an interview as well or better informed about the general subject of their inquiry than the person they wish to interview. There is considerable diversity of opinion over the relative advantages of unstructured as compared with closely structured interviews. The subject for interview is probably the determining factor here, and in many cases a structured interview simply may not be possible, however much desired.

The chief problem for academic researchers in interviewing seems to be the problem of reaching the principals to be interviewed; in some instances this can involve trips of many thousands of miles. A second problem is that many teacher-scholars feel diffident in approaching some of the principals who ought to be interviewed. This quality, or characteristic, varies widely, of course, from person to person, but it is a safe generalization that scholars do not attempt as much interviewing as they might well do because they are often reluctant to approach senior civilian and military personnel to ask them why they did thus and so, or how such-and-such a decision came about, or many other similar fundamental questions which the researcher would like to have clarified. Obtaining access to important and busy people is not always simple, nor always rewarding when it is arranged, but a more imaginative use of, say, former students and alumni or friends of the academician's institution will almost certainly open doors to scholars whose first inclination is to pull back from trying to interview "Mr. Big." A little more of the good reporter's determination to "get the news" would help many academic researchers secure the data they want.

The Use of Questionnaires for Gathering Research Data

Where the scholar is unable personally to interview principals useful to the research he is doing, he may resort to written inquiries. His inquiries may be no more than one or two questions posed in a letter or they may consist of elaborate and detailed questionnaires of many different types. If a number of points need clarification in the research project, or if the researcher wants to obtain the views of a number of people on the same set of questions, he will no doubt develop a questionnaire for the purpose. The techniques involved in the use of questionnaires are becoming highly specialized and in many respects they are, like public opinion polls, a field of research unto themselves.

Many scholars interviewed for this report had a low regard for the use of questionnaires. They pointed out that the people whose opinions they needed to obtain often resisted or completely disregarded questionnaires or gave incomplete and otherwise unsatisfactory answers. It is probably safe to say that many of the persons whose assistance could be of the most value have become antipathetic to questionnaires, and this attitude often wholly defeats the objective in using these instruments. Where groups of people are to be queried, it is clear to most scholars that highly technical and professional skill must be employed in order to construct an adequate questionnaire, evaluate accurately the data obtained, account fairly for the nonrespondents, and handle a host of related sociopsychological problems inherent in this method of collecting data. Asking the right questions is part of the requirement, but asking them in the right way and at the right time may be equally important—factors that may be difficult to control when using written questionnaires.

Even the questionnaire method of data collecting has its financial aspects also, for there is a need for clerical help, for postage, and for supplies, all of which are often well beyond the resources of an individual scholar. The large research centers have been successful in numerous cases in using the questionnaire method, largely because of their greater financial and servicing resources and because of their prestige, which may help persuade persons receiving the questionnaires to respond.

New machines may become increasingly helpful in this area of quantitative research. Such equipment is likely to be found only in the larger institutions, however, and there are several limitations on its use. Planning research in order to utilize mechanical calculators may alter the focus of research in order to "quantify."

Participant-Observation as a Method of Research

A third general method of collecting information to supplement the written record and to gain a better comprehension of the written materials is through participation in, or by close observation of, the conduct of international affairs. This method, of course, limits the researcher to his own lifetime and to activities which he is qualified and able to participate in or is permitted to observe firsthand. In the World War II years a host of academicians participated actively in international affairs at various levels of governmental organization and in a wide variety of activities. Even the academicians who were not full-time official participants had many opportunities for firsthand observation of the unfolding of events of great significance in international affairs. Since the war years many academicians have been in and out of government service of various kinds, making effective use of their participation in public affairs to supplement their previous practical experience and supplement their traditional research methods.

Administrators and academic scholars might well make fuller use of the possibilities of combining useful government service with legitimate personal study and observation for the sake of a subsequent enrichment of their teaching and research. The academician who is helped by his college administration to combine either simultaneously, or *seriatim,* professional service in some governmental, or closely related, activity involving international affairs will not only render a general public service but may also become a more effective member of the institution's faculty. While such arrangements for faculty members often pose problems for administrators, nevertheless in the field of international affairs especially there is a great need for much more of this kind of practical experience and firsthand participation for teachers and scholars. Government research internships for a summer or a year are a partial solution, but actual participation in the full stream of governmental affairs, or the work of private organizations deeply involved in international affairs, is the most rewarding avenue for the scholar.

The Many-Faceted Record: Does It Require Interdisciplinary Research?

Reference has been made to the participation in research in international affairs of persons who have been trained in disciplines other than political science and history, although the body of research in international affairs has been done in these two fields. In the postwar years there has been more and more talk about, and more foundation assistance to, interdisciplinary research. At times it seemed that no research project was well

regarded unless it involved scholars in political science, economics, history, anthropology, and sociology. The popularity of
this organization pattern has abated because it often proved un-
workable. While strictly *inter*disciplinary research has not been
very effective, there has been growing interest in international
affairs research on the part of economists, geographers, and
anthropologists individually, the latter being especially interested
in area studies and in the processes of intercultural relations and
cultural changes. Sociologists and psychologists, however, have
had only slight interest, judging by their response to competitions
for fellowships for area studies[4] and for other research fellowships,[5] and to programs for the training and broadening of research skills for work in the international relations field;[6] and by
the very limited amount of published international affairs research except in the generalized field of area studies.

In the case of area studies it is probably safe to say that there
has been *multi*disciplinary research on a number of world areas
and on certain problems common to all areas, rather than genuine
*inter*disciplinary research as a composite approach and end-
product. The attitude toward even area research by men in
disciplines not at the core of traditional international affairs research has been that of wariness of the selection and of possible
dictation of the subjects and methods of study by those outside
their discipline. Some men in the border disciplines have ques-
tioned the validity of the concept of truly mixed research efforts,
noting that it would take an almost endless amount of time to
"convert" or "educate" all the persons with different disciplinary
training to understand the methods, concepts, and even termi-

[4] See, for example, the report by the chairman on area research training
fellowships (Dr. Philip E. Mosely) of the Social Science Research Council:
"Some Comments on the Experience of the SSRC Program on Area Research
Training Fellowships and Travel Grants," mimeographed for the Second
National Conference on the Study of World Areas, April 6, 1950.

[5] For example, Fulbright fellowships for projects on international relations,
and the new (1956) NATO fellowships.

[6] Ford Foundation International Relations Fellowship Program and the
1956 Summer Research Training Institute on Current Research in International Relations sponsored by the Social Science Research Council.

nology used in research by each discipline, and that this costly effort (in time and money) would likely bear puny fruit once the several-times grafted tree started to produce. They say that it is better that each tree not be tampered with, and that, instead, each discipline should do through its methods what it can do best and let the findings be collated by someone with an over-all international relations interest and training. Collated research findings, however, are not *mixed* research enterprises in the fullest sense of the word.

Perhaps this problem is complicated not so much by a conflict of basic principles as by a lack of experience in such joint interdisciplinary undertakings, as well as by the previously mentioned tendency for academic researchers to work alone with little consultation even with colleagues in their own discipline. Julian H. Steward pointed up this aspect of the problem in developing interdisciplinary research when he wrote: "The problem . . . is whether a group of mature scholars, whose training and research have been rather specialized and whose reputations have been established by their particular contributions to knowledge, are emotionally and intellectually able to alter their research habits to an appreciable degree."[7]

There is another attitude not uncommon among scholars who might do research in international affairs but who refrain from doing so. This is the belief, often propagated by international relations specialists, that the subject matter is so complex that one should not venture into the field unless he is well grounded in history, political science, geography, economics, anthropology, and so on. Since no one has time to become proficient in all or even several of these disciplines, there is a tendency to pull back

---

[7] *Area Research: Theory and Practice* (New York: Social Science Research Council, 1950), p. 18. See also Wendell C. Bennett, *Area Studies in American Universities* (New York: Social Science Research Council, 1951), *passim,* for other comments on area research.

See also the comment by Alexander N. Leighton regarding an interdisciplinary project: "We have been through a number of storms, in which the planks of our interdisciplinary ship have threatened to go back to their various, native forests. . . ." *Items,* II (September 1951), 29.

from doing research in international relations for fear that one's lack of erudition in some discipline will spoil the neat hemline of one's finished research project. Actually, probably no one ever has *all* the tools and preparation he might be expected to have in some ideal concept of the perfect scholar.[8] The objective of "many skills in one skull" is worth working toward, but few scholars will prove to be very successful in this regard. However, two or even three other competencies, or informed understanding of some other disciplines, may well be acquired and will be very helpful.

Evaluation of the Record by the Researcher

However research is organized, and whatever disciplines are brought to bear, the accumulated data from the record, from interviews, and from questionnaires must be evaluated. The methods for evaluating data will vary according to the subject matter and the objective of the study. The methods used may also vary according to the training the researcher has had and in accordance, too, with the resources at his disposal for using different kinds of methods of evaluation.

An intensive content analysis may be one method of evaluating data found in the published record. This may be a fairly tedious procedure and hence an expensive one, in terms of time at least, but it may be an indispensable procedure if the researcher is using data which is uneven in reliability or if he is seeking recurrent basic ideas or attitudes and must perforce check and recheck his material. The content analysis method may have the danger of being overly statistical or quantitative, and insensitive to the nuances of timing and context behind a wide variety of items in the record.

---

[8] The author recalls a long discussion with several faculty members on the subject of requirements for sound biographical research. When all the scholars had made their contributions of "indispensable skills" needed for such work (history, psychology, philosophy, sociology, comparative literature, etc.) it was quite apparent that Plutarch should never have attempted his immortal *Parallel Lives* and that few, if any, subsequent biographers have been really "qualified."

Comparative studies may be another method for evaluating a collection of data for the accuracy and the significance of the information collected. A comparison may be for a given period of time, or it may be a comparison of the same area base over different periods of time. Many other comparative studies or tests are possible for checking information, and, in fact, a perfectionist can continue a research project almost indefinitely if he persists in an endless examination and testing of his sources and data on a variety of comparative bases.

"Case studies" as a form of cross section, or test drilling in depth, may be a method for evaluating a larger body of data to which the case study is germane. The case study in this sense may provide sidelights on the significance, relevance, and even the reliability of data dealing with a general problem of which the case is a specific aspect or portion. Cases for study must be chosen with great care, however, if they are to perform this function of testing or evaluating data broader than the case study.

At all stages the researcher must exercise his judgment as to what facts and data are relevant to his research, what magnitude of importance to assign to different kinds of data, what degree of reliability he can attach to the data he uncovers, and what conclusions or implications he can derive from the data he obtains. How well the researcher does these tasks depends largely on his training, his opportunity and willingness to be "checked" by other qualified scholars, the adequacy of time for careful study, the over-all adequacy of his data, and other considerations. Even if he works in a research center or on an *ad hoc* research team, the primary responsibility for endless judgments rests upon the individual scholar. If he is a conscientious scholar, he will always wonder whether he might not have done better research if only he could have had more material, more information, and more time to check it and evaluate it. The counter-checking of personal judgments and selection of data is an area in which group —or even "grouped"—research will have many rewards for the participants.

Conclusion

In summary, it may be said that there has been considerable experimenting in the postwar years in the organization, methodology, and techniques of research in international relations. Much of this experimenting has been profitable, although there have been some relatively unprofitable enthusiasms, or "fads," such as uncritical endorsement of interdisciplinary research teams. The philanthropic foundations have been generous in their support of experimental and pioneering ventures or proposals for research in this field. This is no doubt one of their proper functions. The pity is that in numerous instances universities which made beginnings on pioneering research with foundation support have not always been able to carry on the enterprise because of lower revenues in the early 1950's or because of the loss of the personnel who initiated the new research program. In methodology there has been some overemphasis on quantitative techniques for a field of study which is unavoidably highly subjective and given to value-directed research. What needs to be stressed is that all methods of research offering some utility to this field ought to be used, and extended arguments over methods or techniques are often wasteful and harmful.

4. The Problem of Access to Materials Needed for Research

To strive, to seek, to find, and not to yield
ALFRED, LORD TENNYSON, *Ulysses*

WHEN A scholar decides to undertake a research project in the field of international affairs, he must first of all give consideration to the availability of necessary materials for the projected research. The nature of his research topic will, of course, have considerable bearing on this problem, as will also the methods of research he intends to employ. In a good many cases, however, the availability or accessibility of materials and other resources needed for his research may determine the methods to be employed in his research.

Access to Foreign Areas

If the researcher, for example, wishes to make a study of some aspect of public opinion in a foreign country or territorial possession, he might prefer to use interviews, observation of group meetings, and study of the mass media of information in that country rather than an analysis of the writings in books, learned journals, and official documents bearing on the topic of his research. He may discover, however, that he cannot even get into the country or the territorial possession of a given country, and he is thereby cut off from interviews, observation, opinion sampling on the spot, and other methods which he might use in developing his study fully. Or he may be able to enter the country, but will find that he cannot get interviews with the influential leaders of public opinion, or will be unable to make a useful sampling of public opinion by questionnaires or other means. Out of many circumstances and conditions limiting what he wants to do will emerge a range of possible research which may be so unpromising as to discourage him from beginning his project, or prove to be so unrewarding as he progresses in his research that he may abandon it. The net effect then may be to force him to limit himself to a few methods of inquiry and fact-finding, and at the worst to frustrate his entire project or force him to alter extensively his intended subject of research.

Historical and legal aspects of international affairs may be studied fairly adequately from the published material in libraries and archives, but even some of this data may be under limitations as to its use or may be located in areas not accessible to an American academic researcher. The most obvious closures of this kind are, of course, the Communist countries of the Soviet Union and mainland China with their satellite states behind the iron curtain and the bamboo curtain. These areas enclose nearly half of the world's population and a large part of the habitable terrain of the globe. There are vast research resources cut off from American scholars in these areas and the loss to our research is immense and serious.[1]

The researcher interested in areas closed to his personal investigation may find some assistance in talking with refugees, escapees, expatriates, and exiles from the country in which he has a research interest. This is of only marginal utility, however, for these people may be able to contribute little or nothing to his particular research project; and if they do have relevant comments or information, there is always the factor of their own traumatic experience having colored their opinion to a degree

[1] See "Area Research Training Fellowships and Travel Grants for Area Research," *SSRC Items,* VI, No. 4, 39, for a report on this problem as it affected the locale of research for SSRC grantees on area research awards. Out of twenty awards for study in China, for example, only five grantees were able to enter that country and "their freedom of movement and inquiry was severely curtailed by events of the civil war."

that would make it of questionable representativeness of what
the people still in the country believe. It is then not so much a
case of what the people or the leaders in a given country think
and believe, to keep to this example, as it is what the expatriate
informer thinks the others think and believe. Other variations
of this alternative are apparent—for example, the use of return-
ing recent visitors to the area concerned. In no case, however, is
the researcher so well equipped to do his project as if he had free
access to the country itself and to the leaders and people of the
country.[2]

The Communist countries and their satellites are not the only
countries or territories which have been closed to American researchers pursuing a project in the field of international affairs.
India, Burma, South Africa, and some other countries have not
welcomed scholars whose research projects dealt with certain
issues of a highly political or controversial character. In other
cases it may be difficult, if not impossible, for an American of
certain racial or religious categories to go to countries where his
race or his religion would override the fact that he is an American citizen, and this would be most conspicuous if his proposed
research dealt with a problem involving his race or his religion,
or a manifestation of either.[3]

A further aspect of this general problem of access to foreign
countries by American academic researchers may be found in the
cases of those scholars and journalists whose previous research
and writing about another country or about some given subject
in public affairs has made them *persona non grata* to the government of the country they would like to visit. It might be interesting to speculate on the extent to which scholars may modify their

[2] Marshall D. Shulman of the Russian Research Center of Harvard has said
that, as regards the study of Soviet foreign policy, "Our information is thinly
supported by inferences from study of the Soviet society through the Soviet
press and literature, impressions of occasional visitors to the Soviet Union, and
interviews with former Soviet citizens." (In a speech at the University of Virginia on February 25, 1956).

[3] Saudi Arabia and other Arab states would not admit an American Jewish
scholar, for example.

actual opinions, when they come to writing up their research, in order not to cut themselves off from a possible return to a country or a subject which they hope to investigate further at a later date. There are some examples of the reverse of this, where fulsome praise of a government or its leaders in published research have been rewarded by decorations, prizes, and awards of honorary citizenship from some governments. There is also the variant on this theme in which an American has made himself a kind of *persona non grata* in America as a consequence of his writing on some controversial issue, and he is thereby cut off from support and even acceptance in America.[4]

The control over where an American researcher may go for his foreign research is not a matter entirely of foreign governmental action. Getting the necessary foreign visa may be no more difficult than getting the American passport authorizing travel to the country in question. In the early postwar period there were numerous limitations on the places abroad which an American, not on official business of the government or one of its instrumentalities, could visit. Japan, for example, was closed for a number of years to persons not officially connected with the occupation forces, and not until 1950 was there a general relaxation of this prohibition. One area after another has been closed to Americans since 1945 and passports have been limited accordingly.[5] These

[4] An illustration of this self-imposed "censorship" on American scholars is the statement in the Preface to *An American Policy in Asia* as follows: "Thus when the Center for International Studies [at Massachusetts Institute of Technology] concluded three years ago [about 1952] that an important service could be performed by launching a fresh examination of the nature of contemporary Communist Chinese society, we decided to assign to the direction of this task a man with no background whatsoever in the China field. *There were many China scholars who in fact would have carried through the analysis with balance and objectivity, but few if any who were not, rightly or wrongly, identified in the public mind with an intemperately stated policy position.*" Italics added. (New York: Technology Press of Massachusetts Institute of Technology and John Wiley & Sons, 1955.)

[5] As recently as early February 1956 Hungary was closed to American citizens by order of the Department of State as a retaliatory measure against actions taken by the government of Hungary against some employees of the American Embassy in Budapest. Albania, Bulgaria, and those portions of China, Korea, and Viet-Nam under Communist control have also been closed to American travelers.

areas may change status (that is, be opened or closed) from time to time depending on conditions in the country and/or our relations with them. Wherever there are war conditions these precautions are of course well advised; in other cases, the soundness of the action is more debatable. If conditions are such that any American lacking diplomatic immunity would likely become involved in serious trouble, there is obviously no wisdom in permitting entry. However, if the prohibition becomes a mechanical or bureaucratic policy, or is a part of the cold war tactics, the loss to learning and thereby to our national intelligence by keeping out qualified researchers may be greater than the risk of some inconvenience to the researcher or the cost to the government of providing him with a reasonable measure of protection.

It should be noted here that our government's recent policy on admitting foreign visitors and immigrants has not put us in a very good bargaining position with governments which might like to exclude American researchers. Our own "curtain" (imposed chiefly through the restrictions of the McCarran-Walter Act) is no mean barrier to many people from many countries. As a partial consequence of our own restrictions, American scholars may have to expect continued restraints by numerous countries upon their desired free entry and to freedom of movement and inquiry if they do obtain entry. American scholars also lose, through this curtain of ours, opportunities to consult with some scholars who might otherwise visit here and confer with them on problems of mutual interest. Overly cautious restrictions on visiting scholars may be a policy as questionable as the restraints upon circulation through the mails of the very valuable *Soviet Press Digest* which scholars rely on for data not easily obtainable otherwise.

The sad truth is that the visitable world for an American scholar doing research in international affairs is much smaller than the actual world. It is even sadder that the areas closed to him are often the ones most important or most promising for research, or are areas about which our government and our people most need more adequate information. International organi-

zations of scholars, such as the International Political Science
Association and the International Sociological Congress, might
well consider this problem and, along with Unesco, study ways
and means of making research more feasible in the world "laboratory" of international affairs.

The Obstacle of Government Security Classifications and Requirements

In an earlier part of this report some attention was given to
the problems many researchers face when they consider going to
remote places where other people and research resources of potential or certain value to them are available. This, it was noted, is
usually a matter of time to make such visits and of money to pay
for the costs of travel, temporary residence away from home, and
some possible related research costs. There is another problem
in the area of access to materials which exists even apart from
time and money. This is the problem of security restraints upon
a great quantity of material which may be at least useful, if not
actually essential, for some research in international affairs.

During World War II the development of security classifications on documentary materials reached a high, and sometimes
extremely complicated, stage of development and regulation. Any
official in almost any department of the government could stamp
or write "Secret" or "Top Secret" (or any other high security
mark) upon almost any material he originated—or even in some
cases on anything which came to his hand previously unclassified.
Once labeled, the document then circulated and was later filed
or possibly destroyed, according to the regulations pertaining to
each security classification as applied in any given agency of the
government at any given time and depending on the degree of
diligence exercised by the persons handling classified material.
This is not the place to discuss this practice (which at times
reached a *reductio ad absurdum* level), except to note that as a
consequence of a general tendency to overclassify information,
an immense amount of informational material was kept from use

of persons outside government when the time came again for peacetime research.[6]

In many agencies so-called "central files" came into possession of only a small part of the total of significant informational material, while individual officers, divisions, and major subunits of agencies kept their own files, either because of physical dispersion[7] or because units and individuals believed they needed substantial files immediately at hand or wanted to control access to such material. In some cases during the war personal correspondence between government officials overseas and their opposite numbers at home developed as a consequence of some apprehension that formal reports and communications were being given to an overly large number of people in government agencies.[8] Most of such private correspondence never went to any central file and rarely left the desk or file of the immediate recipient.[9] When officers were transferred from one job to another, they sometimes sent some of their office files to a central file, but often such materials were destroyed or taken along by the officer. Another practice which deprived the central files, and subsequently the National Archives, of much material of significance to research in international affairs was the practice of some high officers' taking their rather voluminous files with them when they left office. This is a step-down application of the traditional policy of our Presidents' taking their papers with them, despite

[6] In an Associated Press story of July 11, 1956, the historian of the office of the Secretary of Defense, Rudolph A. Winnacher, was quoted as telling a congressional committee that 100,000 file drawers of World War II military papers were stored away under a secrecy classification. See also reports by subcommittee of the House of Representatives Government Operations Committee, released July 28, 1956.

[7] The State Department was housed in over twenty separate buildings in early 1946.

[8] It was not uncommon in the late war years for some messages to be reproduced and sent to literally hundreds of officials in many agencies of the government or to interdepartmental committees, commissions, and joint staffs.

[9] While in the Department of State, 1941–47, the author several times saw correspondence of this kind which contained far more significant information than what was going back and forth in formal cables, dispatches, and instructions, and in memoranda.

the fact that what they handled was the nation's business and not in a literal sense their private business. In some cases efforts were made to enforce regulations against removing classified files by withholding the final paycheck until a sworn statement was made that no property of the government was being taken by the departing officer.[10] This was a belated and not altogether effective check on such losses.

The foregoing discussion has been introduced here because it bears directly on what is in the government files that are open in varying degrees of accessibility to outside researchers. Even when full access is given to certain parts of the central files either on a time-period basis (for example, 1776 up to 1930 in the collection of Department of State files) or certain subjects, there is less in the archives by a good bit than was once in the agency's files or in an office file of someone in the agency.[11] The gaps and the missing papers are often of great significance for balanced research in the international relations of the United States in particular and for other matters also. These gaps may never be filled.

Use of Department of State Files
For Academic Research

Shortly after World War II there was considerable discussion on the use of government files by persons who wanted to do research on the origins, conduct, and objectives of American in-

[10] The author had discussions along this line with some Department of State staff who contended that anything worked on by them was their property. On this basis very little would have been left in central files if all departing officials had taken "their" files with them.

[11] As a small case in point, one may find frequently in the recently printed volumes of *Foreign Relations of the United States* a footnote notation "Not found in Department files," where a particular message or memorandum may have been referred to in the printed text of some official document.

See also the letter from Patrick Hurley to *Life* magazine regarding the memoirs of former President Harry S. Truman: "There is much in these memoirs that is commendable, but the former President's researchers have obviously been somewhat handicapped by the fact that certain secret documents have been removed or stolen from the government files and are no longer available." (*Life,* Feb. 13, 1956, p. 20.)

volvement in that world-wide struggle. The story of World War I was still being written and rewritten (as it will be so long as men are still studying and writing about history and international affairs), and many capable scholars wanted to get to the raw material, the documentary record, which might explain or throw light on very important questions concerning World War II.

In a rather naïve hope—but one that was commendable in spirit—the Rockefeller Foundation in 1946 gave the Council on Foreign Relations a substantial grant to provide a history that would be wholly objective and devoid of "debunking" journalistic characteristics. Access to Department of State files was arranged for the authors of this history, and then the lid blew off. Charles A. Beard, Harry Elmer Barnes, and others protested both the presumed efforts of the Rockefeller Foundation and the Council on Foreign Relations to cut off full review of all the government's actions and failures to act, and to give special preferences to some researchers as against others with respect to access to the files in the official archives of the government.[12] Perhaps as a consequence of this lively controversy the Department of State made more liberal arrangements for outside scholars to have access to its files. Also, great quantities of material were transferred to the National Archives,[13] where their use was controlled by the rules of that agency.

The current[14] policy of the Department of State with respect to nonofficial research in the unpublished records of the Department is set forth in a regulation dated July 8, 1953. This regulation is essentially the same as some earlier provisions governing the use of the files of the Department by outside researchers during the past few years. It is probably as free an arrangement as is consonant with an orderly management of the files, with

[12] See Beard's article in the *Saturday Evening Post* for October 4, 1947, and subsequent press comment on this controversy.

[13] Since December 1949 the National Archives and Records Service is under the supervision of General Services Administration.

[14] As of February 6, 1956. Regulations governing research in the files of the Department of State may be obtained through the Historical Division of the Department.

genuine security requirements, and with the actual needs of qualified researchers.

The Department aims to give inquiring students and other qualified researchers advice and guidance as to the availability of the Department's records within the field of the researcher's interests and also to stimulate and assist research in given areas of American foreign policy and of international affairs by qualified researchers in universities and other research institutions. During fiscal year 1955 advice and assistance were given to 846 outside researchers in connection with requests for access to files of the Department and the review of notes and manuscripts. In the same period of time officers of the Department held conferences in colleges and universities with 125 faculty members and graduate students on various research problems and possible projects.[15]

The Military Establishment has also made efforts to assist qualified scholars in conducting research in the files of the three service departments and in the Department of Defense. The historian of the office of the Secretary of Defense, Rudolph A. Winnacher, supplied the author with regulations pertaining to such research, and others interested would no doubt receive comparable assistance. A circular put out by the Office of the Chief of Military History of the Department of the Army outlines "Opportunities for Research in the Records of the Department of the Army." New regulations are being prepared in all departments on this matter.

When a researcher confronts the immense mortuary of materials now open to him in various government agencies on some subjects[16] for research, he may not be unhappy that much that might be there is not there. On the contrary he may wonder only

[15] Data taken from a memorandum to the author by G. Bernard Noble, chief, Historical Division, Department of State.

[16] An example of a recent subject on which there is abundant research material available is the development of the Marshall plan and the Foreign Assistance Act of 1948, which put the plan into effect on the European side. No major event in recent international relations is so fully documented with data readily found in the United States and in Europe.

how he can possibly digest or even dig through the mountainous mass before him. For many years skilled research workers in the Department of State and in other federal agencies have endeavored to sort out the most meaningful data from all the tons of words piled on an unbelievable amount of paper by tens of thousands of officials reporting, recording, inquiring, and instructing on one or another of innumerable subjects directly or indirectly related to our foreign affairs and to international affairs.

Perhaps the most valuable published effort of this kind is the *Foreign Relations of the United States* prepared by the Department of State somewhat in lieu of an annual report such as most other departments make to the President. For the first one hundred and fifty years of our history the volumes of *Foreign Relations* (and the predecessor publications) were reasonably full and adequate presentations of the major documents exchanged between the Secretary of State and his departmental aides, overseas representatives of the United States, and foreign diplomatic or governmental representatives. Any user of these volumes knows, however, that in recent years (even between 1929 and 1935) the number of footnote notations "not printed" has considerably increased, reflecting the steady increase in the number of documents referred to in the text but not themselves printed. Abstracting of documents has increased and yet, despite the increase in the total number of volumes published each year, there are bigger and bigger gaps in the published record. The volumes have lagged about seventeen years behind current dates, although a strong effort has been made to close this wide gap of years. Special issues of official documents[17] have supplemented the *Foreign*

[17] Beginning in the World War II period with *Peace and War: United States Foreign Policy, 1931–1941,* Department of State Publication No. 1853 (Washington: Government Printing Office, 1942), up to the recent volume on the Yalta Conference (*The Conferences at Malta and Yalta, 1945,* House Document No. 154, 84th Cong., First Sess. [Washington: Government Printing Office, 1955]). An earlier set of publications, Information Series D, 1909–1929, has valuable information for researchers, along with special volumes on disarmament, Far Eastern affairs, history of World War II, etc.

Relations and in a number of cases have brought documents into public view well before they otherwise would have come out on the slow timetable followed since the end of World War II.

There has been much discussion over the delay in the publication of *Foreign Relations of the United States.* The blame certainly lies substantially with the Congress for not appropriating adequate funds for adequate staff to prepare the volumes and to pay the costs of publication. It is interesting to speculate also on how much delay and how many omissions have been caused by officials in other governments, where a document originated with them, or by Department officials who would rather not see some documents published. In our recent panic about the imminent mortal threat to the United States by Communists it has been hazardous for some Foreign Service or Department officers to be revealed in their reports of a decade or more ago as having had a single good word to say for anything Russian, or subsequently even for any Communist-controlled country like Poland or China. If an officer by insight, knowledge, and imagination saw a major trend developing and reported it accurately and then the trend turned out to be a condition or development not popular in America today, the benighted officer who wrote that piece might have to pay with his official head for having reported well, and analyzed events correctly, long before we had a demonstration of the powerful pressure of unrestrained demagoguery on our fears of communism. The net effect of these recent and current fears and of some high-level dismissals "for lack of judgment" has been to make officers wary of what they write now and chary of what they approve for publication, if they get an opportunity to review what they wrote many years ago. Researchers using the files in the Department may also find that after they have collected their notes, these notes may not be approved for quotation, although access to the files was granted by a responsible officer of the Department. This is one of the many ways in which access to all the facts has tended to dry up in recent years. Have we not succeeded, in this respect, only in cutting ourselves off from our own history, and from better understanding of people and events in foreign countries?

When one considers what documentary material is "lost" or closed off to researchers by the guardians of the facts, one also ought to keep in mind that a great amount of the important information for the study of international affairs was never put on paper. In the past twenty years the ease of travel and the speed of travel have made it possible for high officials and staff officials to travel to all parts of the world for personal conversations sometimes completely private and often never recorded or subsequently reported. From the time President Franklin D. Roosevelt went to Buenos Aires in 1936, heads of state and the leading officials in foreign offices,[18] defense ministries, and other agencies involved in international affairs have been flying around the world. Conferences and international organizations by the thousands annually have made possible private consultations among government officials which in an earlier generation were rare events. Telephones and "telecom" conversations have displaced much that once went by cable or by letter, and a great quantity of important talk, including major discussions, is never recorded or is summarized only briefly and often not too accurately. So, despite a vast increase in the total bulk of paper records, less and less of the whole record is to be found in official papers. Sometimes important information about official conversations is recorded, however, in the personal diaries or letters of the principals and may later be revealed in published form, as in *The Forrestal Diaries,* for example.

Significance for Researchers of New Procedures in Diplomacy

What do the developments in more direct personal contact at high levels of international intercourse mean to the academic

---

[18] See for instance the map of Secretary Byrnes' travel by boat and by air appearing in the inside cover of his book, *Speaking Frankly*. Secretary of State John Foster Dulles has flown more than any other Secretary of State.

researcher? Is it significant to the future of research by those who may have little or no exposure to government workings and may still believe that they can "look at the record" in a literal way? What does it mean in terms of training graduate students for future research in international affairs, in whose foreseeable lifetime there will be many restraints upon free access to materials in foreign countries, in our country, and even in international agencies? These are not idle questions, and they merit more discussion than may be given to them here. They deserve the careful attention of researchers, teachers of graduate students, college and university research directors, government officials, and the public at large.

The author ventures a few comments on these questions in the hope that other persons will be stimulated to think more critically about the problems posed. The comments which follow relate to some previous observations on research methods, on training for research, and on the needs for travel to supplement reading. At the risk of some repetition but for a different focus the following comments may be in order here.

First of all, it would seem that the old ideal of gathering all the documents, reading all the published papers, the secondary sources, and other relevant printed material may not be feasible for a big problem or major development since 1940. In some cases, depending on the research topic, much of the story may be found in documents and other published sources which are readily accessible. In other cases, however, a good part of the story may be found in such sources, but only after considerable delay in time and with considerable difficulty in obtaining access to materials. In still other cases, including some of the most vital problems in our international affairs (for example, relations with the Soviet Union and with Communist China), it may never be possible to use a substantial body of documentary material either because no access will be permitted to Americans seeking to study records in the Soviet Union or in Communist China, or even our own records, or because no published or written records will exist for many of the most vital discussions and decisions.

By the device of much reading in a very wide variety of publications it is possible to fill in some of the gaps in the official
records that are published or are open to academic researchers.
This is tedious work, however, and it requires access to many
periodicals which not even the largest libraries will be able to
supply in full. The scholar is forced to draw deductions from
piecemeal data and then check and countercheck with care and
patience.

The academic researcher in international affairs may be
tempted to go back for a time—perhaps for a long time—to investigating either events of pre-World War II for possible present
and future significance, or to studying the subjects on which
there are few barriers of access to needed materials. There is
work aplenty to be done here: in the processes of governments
at all observable levels of action; in the processes of international
bodies; in the perennial and nearly universal problems of the
care of refugees (of whom there will surely be many more in
this century); in the impact of technology upon nature and mankind; and numerous other subjects of varying degrees of suscep-
tibility to free and uninhibited investigation and reporting. If a
researcher ventures into a field where the records are fragmentary
or where access to individuals is limited and answers are decep-
tive, it is to be hoped at least that he will not claim that he has
"read all the documents" or has "all the facts" (when such is
clearly impossible) and thereby make academic research look
more myopic than it often is.[19]

Some Adaptations and Improvisations Needed To Meet the Problem of Access to Materials

The training of researchers in the future may call for schooling
in a variety of research techniques, instead of grinding along on
the old practice of a detailed, exhaustive (and often exhausting)

[19] One good consequence of the inadequacy of reliable printed sources on
some topics may be to reduce the proliferation of footnotes which in the
Germanic manner has often been mistaken in this country, too, for good
research, when it was often just stirring up the sediment at the bottom to
obscure how little was at the top.

analysis of some little topic no one else has seen fit to study, or a rehash of an old topic in such a very different way as to make it qualify as "a contribution to new knowledge."[20] It may well prove to be more important to concentrate on training a student to use different research techniques skillfully so that he can adjust to whatever conditions he finds prevailing when he subsequently begins his self-directed research. Requiring a student to work away with one method may not help him in later years half so much as teaching him how to adjust methods to fit a variety of difficult research situations. If files are closed, interviewing of former and present participants may be the only sound procedure for a given project; if interviewing is impossible and files are closed or limited, indirect research by deduction from analogies may be the next best procedure, and so on. Each device or technique requires training and guided practice in its use.[21]

The researcher who has been essentially based at a college or university but who goes in and out of government (national or international) will have to cope with a different phase of this general problem of access to materials. There will be for him the question of what he can say, at what time, on which subjects within his government experience, and at what possible consequence to himself as regards his future employment by the government or access to a foreign country previously within his field of responsibility while in government. He too may find that he can't quote chapter and verse from certain documents (even though they may have been originated by him) and he can speak only in broad statements and ask his readers to believe him because he was "there," so to speak. The reader, unable to check

[20] In the preface to the 1949 edition of *Doctoral Dissertations in Progress in History* the executive secretary of the American Historical Association exhorted students to avoid duplications in subjects (there were about one thousand *titles* listed), and he noted some persistent duplications, first spotted in the 1947 dissertation census (Washington: American Historical Association).

[21] See C. Dale Fuller, *Training of Specialists in International Relations* (Washington: American Council on Education, 1957) for some comments on the question of diversified graduate training.

the documents, can then only wonder how skilled an observer, reporter, and analyst this writer is who asks his statements to be taken on faith rather than checked against actual documents or records. Writing by these ex-participants will often not be in the "memoirs" category, but they will border on that and may be as much literary as documentary.

One way in which an academic researcher who is severely limited in travel funds and travel time can augment his access to people in order to obtain the information he needs, is to do all he can to arrange for these people to visit his institution. Such visitors can often be brought to the campus to meet with classes, seminars, public affairs discussion clubs or student groups, or for public or semipublic lectures and forums. It is apparent from many interviews on this matter that scholars have not used all the imagination and initiative which they might have used in bringing resources for research to their campuses in the form of visiting speakers. Many governments welcome invitations addressed to their embassies or consulates for officials or their nationals who may be visiting in the United States, to go to college and university centers. These governments know that the academic community is often a center of influence in the larger public and that hence it is a good point of contact for these governments with Americans. Officials of our own government also often welcome chances to make or renew academic contacts.

Among private citizens there is a virtually untapped "gold mine" of available persons who are rarely called upon by academic researchers as they could be. Visiting Fulbright scholars and students from foreign countries, representatives of firms doing business abroad, and members of all kinds of private organizations with foreign activities are a few examples in this category. As said the King in *The King and I* there are etceteras in quantity to be added to this method of obtaining access to people with actual or potential information of much value to a researcher who plans his utilization of such resources as carefully as he scans the printed record. The officials or even the private citizen will often be more communicative if he is consulted away from his office. He is likely also to take a more lively interest in the scholar's work when he is away from his own work. The problem of access to materials needed for research offers a challenge almost as exciting in some instances as the subject under research and the findings resulting from research.

5. The Outlets and Uses for Academic Research in International Affairs

Man dwells apart, though not alone,
He walks among his peers unread

JEAN INGELOW (1820–97)

AS NOTED earlier in this report (especially chapter 2), one of the major uses of research is in the enrichment of a scholar's teaching. The research effort as well as the actual research findings invigorate any scholar, and he therefore acquires more enthusiasm for learning as well as more knowledge. He takes much more to his students as a consequence of his own research. There is virtually no disagreement in this belief that a scholar, like a gardener, must dig in the field of knowledge if he is going to make that garden yield something of value to his students, his colleagues, and the great community of mankind. The more specialized courses in colleges and universities often seem to be the chief beneficiaries of an academic scholar's research. Such specialized courses may, in fact, often appear to be the reason for research, and also the courses are often the result of specialized research. The fact is, however, that even the more general courses in the field of international affairs and the general public are often the beneficiaries of the research that may have been done originally with publications or a particular advanced course in mind. The scholar's findings if circulated not only to his students, who become carriers of his ideas, but also to a wider audience through publication and lectures frequently will find uses far removed from their original objective.

The Publication of Research Findings

The importance of publication, or at least wide circulation, of research findings has two facets. One facet is the satisfaction a researcher experiences when he sees his research work rewarded by a wider circulation of his findings and ideas than he can give to them orally. The other facet is the need of other people to learn more about every aspect of international affairs and to apply, wherever possible, the findings of research efforts. Publication media and outlets are, therefore, the capillaries of the literate community which carry the nourishment of new information and new ideas to all the members of society who can and who will accept this reinvigoration.

In the prewar (pre-1940) period there were numerous outlets or media for circulation of the scholar's research findings in international affairs. Various journals of professional and learned societies were either wholly devoted to international affairs, such as the *American Journal of International Law,* or carried a substantial number of articles on international affairs subjects—for example, the *American Political Science Review,* the *Political Science Quarterly, Annals of the American Academy of Political and Social Science,* and other similar periodicals. Opportunities for publication were provided in other journals supported by research centers (*Foreign Affairs* of the Council on Foreign Relations); or by foundations (*International Conciliation* of the Carnegie Endowment for International Peace); or by private organizations (the *American Scholar* of the Phi Beta Kappa fraternity); or by universities, notably the *Yale Review* and the *Virginia Quarterly,* and by private subscription membership groups, such as the "Headline Books" and "Foreign Policy Reports" of the Foreign Policy Association. In the prewar or early wartime years there were numerous specialized "area" journals such as the *Inter-American Quarterly* (once the *Quarterly Journal of Inter-American Relations*) and other journals devoted to the Pacific area, the Far East, or to subject specialties in economics, international organization, and so on. The scholarly journals were reasonably plentiful for the publication needs of the researchers. Journals of the several historical associations and journals in economics have also carried a good quantity of research in international affairs. Several publications had difficulty meeting their costs of operation in the war years and occasionally one dropped out of publication, like the *Inter-American Quarterly*, for lack of adequate financial support.

In the commercial trade field there were many publication outlets in periodicals, such as *Current History*, which had good standing, and in some newspapers, like the *New York Times Sunday Magazine*, which were accepted by scholars as respectable outlets for serious research. The *Readers' Guide to Periodical Literature* and the *International Index to Periodicals* directed readers to the more popular and to the more scholarly publications respectively (as they still do) and they reflected the rather large number of outlets for publication of research findings in international affairs. Foreign periodicals, scholarly and commercial, offered numerous outlets also.

Book publishers, university presses, and commercial presses offered many opportunities but even by 1940 the costs of book publication were climbing beyond the range of returns from sales for many scholarly studies, and a demand was growing for more subsidized university presses or more funds to pay commercial guarantees for the costs of publication. Cheap editions of books on scholarly subjects by contemporary writers had not become readily available in America. The "Modern Library" and "Pocket Books" showed a trend toward serious books[1] in the early 1940's. Book publishing was often more easily arranged abroad, but the subjects, of course, had to appeal to the foreign publisher unless he too had a guarantee of a return on his publication costs.

In the postwar period there have been some notable and al-

[1] See Allan Nevins and Henry Steele Commager, *The Pocket History of the United States* (New York: Pocket Books, 1943) as an example.

most revolutionary developments regarding the media for the circulation of research findings. The prewar journals, with very few exceptions, have persisted and some have increased in size, and among those not solely devoted to international affairs almost all have revealed a considerably increased interest in and attention to such research. In addition to the older journals, numerous new journals have appeared since 1945.

World Politics, a quarterly journal devoted to international affairs, is one of the major newcomers to this field along with the *World Affairs Interpreter* (recently renamed the *World Affairs Quarterly*). Other specialized journals for areas like the Middle East, Asia, and Africa have made their appearance in recent years. New subject-oriented journals have also appeared, dealing with problems in the field of economic development and cultural change, the prevention of war, the international exchange of persons, and other subjects. Commercial publications, even of the "slick" and "popular" categories, have made increasing use of solid academic research in international relations, and at the same time they have shown a marked increase of journalistic reporting and editorial commentary on international affairs.

All journals and periodicals have their ups and downs in terms of the amount of copy in hand worthy of publication; the quantity as well as the quality of manuscripts offered will often vary in accordance with the energy, boldness, personal contacts, and general skill and prestige of the editorial staff of a journal or periodical. Having talked with editors of periodical publications, ranging from those who have been interested in publishing only international affairs research to those whose interests are only occasionally concerned with international affairs, the author believes one can safely say that no good article on international affairs is unable to find a suitable journal for its publication. There are pieces, to be sure, going from one editor to another, but simply because they have been written and submitted for publication is no assurance or reason that they should necessarily be published. Some of what is offered for publication has no utility for operational use or for a genuine increase of the store of significant knowledge. In fact, a considerable amount of what has been published would never have been missed if it had not appeared in printed form.

New Means for the Publication and Distribution of Research

In the course of the war many new processes were developed, and some old ones were perfected, for making quickly and cheaply dozens or hundreds of copies of typewritten or photo-offset papers. The demands of government agencies for more copies of more usable quality than could be obtained by carbon copies or tedious and often messy mimeographing led to many of these new developments. New reproductive materials, new machines, chemically treated papers, photographic devices, all contributed to meet the demands of the government and subsequently to serve the needs of scholars also.

Research findings and others writings which would not justify the costs of printing in journals or pamphlets now find wide distribution in various forms of multi-processing or photo-duplication. In some cases the author may in fact prefer that his research not be as widely circulated as would be the case with a major journal. He may prefer that only one hundred people more or less should see his product, after which distribution he may revise it and offer it for wider publication. It is interesting to speculate on the degree to which ideas and new data have been given currency and use by the medium of these relatively cheap and rapid means of duplication and the extent to which they have been a substitute for old-style publication.

In between the multi-processed material and the printed journal article or book has been the device of substantial "memoranda" with sturdy paper covers and contents multilithed by some process less expensive than printing but more attractive and durable than most ordinary multi-copy processes. The Yale

Institute for International Studies made exceptionally good use of the memorandum device, and many of the same group who were at Yale have carried on that practice for the last few years from the Princeton Center for International Studies. The Organizational Behavior Section of the Foreign Policy Analysis Project at Princeton University has also used the memorandum device in the same letter-size format of the old Yale series and the Princeton Center's series. The Princeton Center for Research on World Political Institutions has put out "Interim Papers" from time to time since 1953 which have been of memorandum size. Other institutions and research centers are using this device, and it will undoubtedly become even more popular for it is a convenient and attractive form of presentation for research findings. There are many who believe that memoranda of this kind, convenient to read and to file, are more widely perused in and outside government than would be true if the memoranda had appeared as articles in the more standard journals in this field.

One great advantage to the user of this type of publication is its separateness (for purposes of filing or for class assignments, and the like) and its considerable sturdiness without the cost of a better bound publication. It no doubt has also made possible the publication of parts of a research project in piecemeal stages without waiting for completion of the entire project which may finally appear in book form. For those who believe in that old saying that "most books should have been only magazine articles, and many articles should never have been published," the memorandum or brochure is a happy middle ground. Memoranda so published, *seriatim* with no fixed schedule of releases, have a great advantage over a quarterly or other time-bound publication in that the editor of the former may pick and choose carefully while the editor of the latter is apt to be like a beetle pinned to a board in his need to get a full issue out on schedule. The memorandum is a promising descendant of the ancient family of printed pamphlets and booklets, and it will likely have a useful role for a long time.

One disadvantage of the memorandum device is that, unlike articles in the major journals, they are not indexed in guides to periodicals. They also will not likely appear in guides to or bibliographies of recent books, and hence they tend to be very limited in their circulation. Having been issued in small number, they may more easily be lost to general use as time goes by, in contrast again with journal articles or the ordinary book or monograph. These are not insuperable disadvantages, however.

The Problem of Book Publishing for Scholarly Research

As book publishing costs have increased in the postwar period, many researchers have complained that they have had difficulty finding book publishers who are willing to take manuscripts without sizable guarantee unless the subject of the research was of very timely interest and fairly wide appeal. At some institutions scholars have urged expansion of university presses despite the financial difficulties they often have encountered. While pressures for university presses have usually been strongest from scholars in the humanities (and there have been many scholars in these disciplines who were doing research related to international affairs), there has also been some urging from scholars in the social sciences, where international affairs research is more common. University presses are clearly beyond the financial resources of many institutions, and in the past few years of lean income and high operating costs there has been no responsive support from administrators to pleas for more publishing facilities on the campus. Of some assistance was the Ford Foundation grant of $1,725,000 in 1957 to university presses for a five-year program to support and stimulate publication in the humanities and the social sciences.

One substitute for a university press is an interuniversity press based on the voluntary membership and pro-rated costs of membership among several institutions. For a good many years this concept has been investigated and discussed by the Southern University Conference (an organization of about fifty leading col-

leges and universities in the fourteen Southern states) but nothing
has come thus far of this effort.[2] The arguments for pooling interests and funds in an interuniversity press include (*a*) avoiding
business inefficiency, (*b*) overcoming the very small list of titles
for a single press, and (*c*) the lack of an adequate sales force; all
these limitations pertain to many single-institution university
presses. The conference has not succeeded in obtaining foundation support or even adequate guarantees of financial support
from its own members, some of whose institutions already have
university presses. Such cooperation may come about in the future but other developments in the commercial book field make
it seem rather unlikely.

The "Pocket Book" and other cheap paper-bound reprint
series have moved increasingly into the field of new books on important nonfiction subjects in recent years. As this development
has taken place, there has been increasing experimentation in the
publication of inexpensive, paper-bound books of solid scholarly
content. The Doubleday "Short Studies in Political Science" is
one such venture and its series already includes several books in
the field of international affairs,[3] no one of which sells for more
than one dollar, but every one of which is neatly printed and
adequately bound with a tough paper cover.

More publishers will certainly initiate similar series, especially
where the books show some promise of being adopted as texts or
supplementary reading in college and university courses in international affairs, which are now beginning to grow in size after
the 1951–55 slump. Some university presses have been able to
produce attractive small books with scholarly research findings at
prices of one dollar or slightly more. The Stanford University
Press publications of the Hoover Institute Studies are excellent
examples of this development,[4] as are also the publications of the

---

[2] See *Proceedings . . . Southern University Conference,* 1954, pp. 88–91.

[3] See for example the second number in this series, *The Revolution in
American Foreign Policy, 1945–1954,* by William G. Carleton of the University
of Florida (Garden City, N.Y.: Doubleday & Co., 1954), 94 pp., $0.95.

[4] See for example a recent number in the series of Hoover Institute Studies,

Princeton University Press for the Princeton Center for Research on World Political Institutions.[5] Bigger markets for inexpensive books and new developments in printing processes may conceivably be the combination which will make it possible for more short books to be published and to reach a wider audience than ever before. The needs of adult education in world affairs may add substantially to the market for the short and cheap books by good scholars.

The publication of collections of short papers in book form has been desired by scholars for a long time, but such collections often do not sell well and even a learned journal must be careful of venturing too often into the publication of symposia of several articles on a single subject.[6] If foundations would more often provide funds to facilitate the publication of research findings, more general benefit probably would be realized from the grants they make for research. On the other hand, unless some reliable agency or third party applies sound critical and editorial judgment to determine what merits publication, the foundations might find themselves only adding to the already full flood of published material, not all of which merits the cost in time and money for publication and distribution. Wide distribution of multi-processed reports or of printed extracts, or even the provision of microfilm copies of research findings might be the wisest middle course of action for foundations to support. In this manner valuable research work would not lack for some considerable circula-

---

The Communist Revolution: An Outline of Strategy and Tactics, by Harold H. Fisher (Stanford, Calif.: Stanford University Press, 1955), 89 pp., $1.00.

[5] See Publication No. 4 ("Multiple Loyalties . . ." by Harold Guetzkow) as an example, and for a list of other Center publications.

[6] The experience of the *Journal of Politics* of the Southern Political Science Association has verified this rather hazardous concentration on special issues or single subjects for a single regular issue.

On the other hand the *Annals* of the American Academy of Political and Social Science has followed the practice of concentrating individual issues on one general subject. In the trade field this practice has been followed by *Current History* and to a considerable degree recently by *The Atlantic,* with special country supplements. Other "specializers" are *International Conciliation* and the *Journal of International Affairs.*

tion and use, but the high costs of printing and other publishing costs would be avoided. Some foundation grants in recent years have provided for distribution of research findings in the various inexpensive forms described above.

Scholars in the field of foreign affairs might consider the potentialities of a better use of radio and television to make known their research findings. For many years several institutions have presented radio roundtables or forums on topics of current interest at which scholars have worked into the discussion some aspects of their scholarly research. Television offers the added advantage that the listener is also a watcher in the unseen audience and that research material which is based on charts, pictographs, and other visual presentations can be brought out more effectively than if the presentation were only by radio. Scholars and organizations particularly devoted to research in international affairs ought to explore more fully the possibilities for their research comparable to what medical researchers have been able to do recently in the television program *Medical Horizons*. Edward R. Murrow on his *See It Now* has demonstrated that a carefully prepared program on international affairs will draw an immense audience.[7]

A little more boldness and increased willingness on the part of scholars to popularize their research may be an essential first step before the necessary financing can be found to present expensive televised education of this kind. The University of Denver has used its Social Science Foundation staff for some encouraging pioneering in this field, and has produced a weekly program which crowds the popular entertainment programs for top listener support. The foundation has also experimented with a summer (1955) workshop for training teachers in the use of mass media

[7] A classic of this type of program was Murrow's presentation of on-the-spot interviews with French people concerning their attitudes toward the proposed European Defense Community. A similar program could have incorporated the research findings of some of our academic scholars who have studied intensively the basis and quality of postwar French public opinion on European integration proposals.

for world affairs education. If scholars are going to contribute substantially to increased public understanding of areas of the world or of problems in international relations outside the educational experience of a great majority of the American people, then they must themselves help to build the foundation of public education through basic popular books and increasingly through the mass media of the press, radio, and television.[8] If scholars fail to do their part and through their research write only for each other or talk only to each other, they will have little or no justification for berating the public for following the lead of demagogues or ill-informed politicians who think they are offering programs and policies in our foreign relations that will be suitable to public opinion. The need for improvement of communication between scholars and those charged with operating the government is great and urgent, but the need for academicians to educate the public is perhaps greater.[9]

Use by Governmental Agencies of Academic Research in International Affairs

In approaching the question of the use of academic research by governmental agencies one is of course confronted first of all by the impossibility of measuring use. So many considerations enter into the final determination of policy and the shaping of actions to implement policy that it would be a brave soul indeed who would venture to say that out of a total of X amount of information and guidance a given portion came from academic research, and another given portion came from outside, nonacademic, and nongovernmental sources, with still other portions from internal

[8] The Conference on Southern Asia Studies (sponsored by the Joint Committee on Southern Asia of the American Council of Learned Societies and the Social Science Research Council) included discussion of this problem at a meeting at the University of Pennsylvania, December 2–4, 1949. See *Proceedings* of the conference (hectographed), p. 8.

[9] See the study on adult education in world affairs by Cyril O. Houle and Charles A. Nelson, *The University, the Citizen, and World Affairs,* "Studies in Universities and World Affairs" (Washington: American Council on Education, 1956), especially pp. 145–66 on the need for university subject specialists to make more effort to bring their knowledge to the general public.

government sources and from within the individual officers' own intuition, hunches, or perversities. Some degree of measurement may be undertaken, however, by dividing the problem into smaller parts.

First of all it should be noted that most of the officer personnel in the agencies of our government dealing with international affairs and the personnel in international agencies who have policy-making or responsible positions have had advanced education, many at our best institutions of higher learning.[10] Obviously if what was said earlier about research being reflected in better teaching was valid, and if a high percentage of the officers in the Department of State, other departments and agencies of the government, and the Foreign Service of the United States have had a very considerable amount of education, then much of the fruit of research in international affairs has been carried bodily into government service by these college and university-trained individuals. The instruction which officials received while in college often guides them for many years, and the habits of study and work they acquired in colleges and universities may shape their working habits for most, if not all, of their careers. Some students may in fact literally take with them the books and journals they used in college and, for a while at least, keep them handy as they wrestle with the problems of their new profession.

Having had, as a group, a rather exceptional amount of higher education it is to be expected, but not always realized, that officers in the government handling international problems will turn as often as they can to the reading of the journals which deal with the subject matter of their work. If they deal with problems of a particular geographic area, they may read journals specifically devoted to that area; if they deal with subject fields, such as international finance, or transportation, for example, they may

[10] See James L. McCamy and Alessandro Corradini, "The People of the State Department and the Foreign Service," *American Political Science Review*, XLVIII (December 1954), 1076. See also McCamy, *The Administration of American Foreign Affairs* (New York: Knopf, 1952), pp. 92–94 and 192–95 for an analysis of an earlier group of our foreign affairs officials.

seek out the journals which help them most with their immediate interests. The same is true, of course, of pamphlets, booklets, and even for books—although rarely is time sufficient to read books in addition to the plethora of pages pushed along on the government's own information belt. The mail carts that go the rounds of the offices in the Department of State and other agencies working on foreign affairs often carry the research work of academic scholars in the forms noted above. The libraries of these agencies may not be crowded with readers, but the delivery of journals, pamphlets, and books runs high. Greater use of academic research findings will of course be prevalent in the research and intelligence offices than will be the case in the average action desk, where the pressure is on drafting, approving, or reading the internal communications that make up the lifestream of the government. As noted earlier, there is a marked tendency also for government officials to favor reading what appears to be especially designed for them or what has apparent limited circulation, such as some of the memoranda series mentioned or comparable special reports for the government.

In addition to what the government workers bring with them as part of their education, and in addition to what they voluntarily seek on an individual basis in the published output of academic research, there is of course the planned procurement of academic research referred to earlier. Various agencies of the government have made contracts with academic institutions and with individuals at academic institutions to undertake research on specified subjects and occasionally on basic research pertinent to the problems of international affairs. Several agencies, notably the Department of State (through its External Research Staff) and the Central Intelligence Agency, endeavor to keep informed on what research is being done at academic centers. These agencies make known in the government what is being done outside and frequently they obtain for government use copies of unpublished research findings to supplement what has already been published or what has been contracted for by the government agencies. The materials sought by these agencies include master's theses and doctoral dissertations as well as the research work of more advanced scholars.

To return to the question "how much?" it is probably safe to say that not enough use is being made of academic research but that it is difficult to see how more use might be achieved easily. If a central abstracting and indexing service were established, there would no doubt be more use of academic research in government circles, but this would be a tedious and expensive enterprise and of dubious value unless the abstracts were fairly lengthy. The problem here is the old bogey of not having time enough in government to read all that might be helpful before action must be taken. The time for reading and reflection is much too limited for the officials charged with major responsibility.

The research findings of the academicians can be useful to government personnel not only for the factual data the findings may reveal, or just for an ordering of the facts around some hypothesis, theory, or conjecture, but in addition they can help an official develop his feel for the action problem he has to consider. It may be that he can benefit most by talking with a research scholar or a group of scholars whose attention has been focused intently and perhaps without distractions on the very same issue or specific problem facing the official. The Brookings Institution seminars in American foreign policy (about fourteen meetings from 1948 through 1952) seemed to serve this purpose very effectively in that government officials often spent several days in close association with research scholars discussing current issues in American foreign relations. Much more along this line could be done and the Brookings seminars have been adopted by several universities, with generous foundation support.

Besides the acquisition of new information and the development of a better feel for international affairs problems, the government official may also learn from the academic scholar how to analyze more effectively the issues which the government faces. The government official may be the beneficiary, in a very economical way, of the discovery of effective analytical techniques and tools which the scholar after much time and with much trial and error has finally perfected in his research methods and work. With new but tested analytical tools the government officials and agencies can, in effect, ride into battle on the shoulders of scholars who have trod the hard ground of experimentation and probing with case studies and theoretical models.

One of the major difficulties in augmenting the collaboration between the government person as user of research and the scholar as producer of research findings is that they very often approach their work with very different objectives and needs in mind. The operator (whether in government or in international business) is confronted by a succession of problems forcing action decisions (among which may be the decision not to act), and he is interested in knowledge for its *use* in solving current problems. The researcher, on the other hand, may be preoccupied with finding out the nature of the problem, the *why* of the problem, and he may have comparatively little interest in solving the problem because that is not his responsibility. Even with these different attitudes toward the same problem, it is possible, however, for the researcher to be very helpful to the practical operator if in the course of research there are questions raised, if alternative lines of action are explored, and if possible consequences of action or inaction are subjected to critical speculation by the scholar. The researcher can leave the problem unsolved and still have performed a useful service if he has stirred the operator to think in a broader way.

Academic researchers are apt to move more slowly, be more painstaking and more theoretical than are government officials. Because academic research is often slow work, it is costly, and some government personnel may question whether the delay and expense involved in contract research pay off in the final research product. Conversely the scholar is often irritated and frustrated if he is pushed to find usable "answers."

Most of the foregoing discussion has focused on the use of academic research in international affairs by government agencies, including by inference at least non-American governments and also international governmental bodies. Much of what has been said on this matter applies to the use of academic research by private organizations, businesses, and individuals with international interests and operating problems. Vast quantities of potentially useful research are not drawn upon by such proper "customers" because the customers often do not know about the research, or it is written in language not easily understandable to them, or they are too pressed and preoccupied with immediate tasks to take time to do the reading or the consulting with scholars that could simplify or clarify their operating needs.

Conclusion

Two general features concerning the use of academic research in international affairs stand out. First, it is clear that a great portion of research activity never comes to a point of completion where it can be used easily by others unless the researcher expounds it in lectures or in private conversations. Many engines are running, so to speak, but a lot of the research energy never gets put into gear to turn any wheels except the researchers' and those of a few students or associates. There is a debatable question as to whether research can be considered completed unless it is made available in some form to all who might want to use it. The administrators who put heavy emphasis on *published* research are to this extent acting as catalysts to bring the research effort to its full and proper conclusion. The pressure to publish, however, has no doubt forced a vast quantity of research into print before it was fully ready for publication.

A second feature concerning outlets and uses for academic research is that in very recent years there has been a marked improvement in both respects. Many more media are now available to scholars to obtain wide circulation for their research at a fairly low cost. Possibly as a consequence of this development, there is undoubtedly a much wider use of academic research by governments of nations and by nongovernmental bodies now than before 1940. The war experience, which brought together many career operators and career scholars, did much to promote the increased use of academic research in the war and postwar years. Each group, as a consequence of this experience, has a better idea of what the other needs to know in order to do a given job. The only cloud over this generally fortuitous experience has been the requirement for security clearances and security controls on research findings. This restraining effect on a wider and freer association between personnel in government, and even business, and the scholars has been unfortunate.

The needs of governments for more social science research in general have increased markedly in recent years, and as a part of this general need there has been a marked increase of use by governments of social science research including research in international affairs.[11] The *need* will increase; it is to be hoped that ways will be found to augment the use of academic research— both independent and contract—by government agencies.

[11] For a good discussion of this problem see Milton D. Graham, *Federal Utilization of Social Science Research: Exploration of the Problems* (Washington: Brookings Institution, August 1954). There is a full account in this preliminary paper of the consideration by Congress of social science research under government auspices, both in and outside the National Science Foundation, and a report on the amount of research in the social sciences supported by the Federal Government.

See also the periodic reports of the National Science Foundation.

6. Some Subjects for Research in International Affairs

Something lost behind the ranges,
Something lost and waiting for you—
Go and seek it; go and look behind the ranges.

R. Kipling, *The Explorer*

WHAT are the areas or topics for research which have received major attention among academic researchers in the decade 1945–55?

A discussion of the above question could easily lead to a detailed inventory of published research since the end of World War II. This is not the purpose of this study, as was noted in chapter 1, and the comments which follow will, therefore, be editorial in nature.

As mentioned previously, the Carnegie Endowment for International Peace published four comprehensive inventories of current research in international affairs for the period 1947–51. Many of the projects reported in the first inventory had been initiated before 1947, and also the inventory published in early 1952 no doubt included projects that carried on into 1953 or even later; thus, the total time spread for these four inventories is a good part of a decade. Another ready source of information on who was doing what research in international affairs in much of the 1940's is the recent bibliography prepared under the auspices of the Council on Foreign Relations, *Foreign Affairs Bibliography: A Selected and Annotated List of Books on International Relations, 1942–1952* compiled by Henry L. Roberts.[1] A partial supplement to the

[1] New York: Harper & Bros., 1955.

Roberts bibliography is the list of books published in the annual volumes of the council entitled, *The United States in World Affairs*[2] for the years since 1952, and also in the other bibliographies and guides to published research which have been referred to or are to be found in the bibliography at the end of this report.

In the decade after World War II there were some rather significant shifts in research emphasis in scholarly research in international affairs. Some of these changes in emphasis no doubt grew out of the war experience, and others quite possibly represented a drying-up of interest or a belief that a particular subject had been worked over adequately. As an example of the former, one finds an increased interest in foreign policy and policy making. As illustration of the latter change of emphasis one finds a rather sharp dropping-off in purely legal studies such as case studies of international boundary disputes and similar legal controversies.[3] This latter change reflects, no doubt, a general disillusionment with the role and efficacy of international law in resolving contemporary international conflicts. Many college teachers became cynical, or skeptical at least, about the adequacy of formal international law for such purposes and turned from it as a subject to which they could give enthusiastic research attention. In the study of current academic research in 1950 made by Hawley and Dexter[4] only 21 studies were on the subject of international law (excluding the United Nations) out of a total of 308 studies in the field of international relations. Other evidence of this trend away from international legal studies may be found in the current bibliographies in *Foreign Affairs,* the *American Political Science*

[2] New York: Harper & Bros.

[3] The decline of interest in research into legal disputes in Latin American affairs is apparent in Harry Kantor, *A Bibliography of Unpublished Doctoral Dissertations and Master's Theses Dealing with the Governments, Politics and International Relations of Latin America* (Gainesville, Fla.: Inter-American Bibliographical and Library Assoc.), Series I, Vol. 13 (1953).

[4] Claude E. Hawley and Lewis A. Dexter, "Recent Political Science Research in American Universities," *American Political Science Review,* XLVI (June 1952), 474.

Review, and similar journals. While there was a dropping-off, or at best a leveling-off, of research interest in international law topics, there was a very marked growth in research in 1945–55 on many aspects of international organization. The creation of the United Nations and the many specialized bodies related to it, the reorganization of the inter-American system, the emergence of new regional organizations in the Caribbean, in the South Pacific, in Europe, in the Far East, and in the military sphere gave a tremendous impetus to research in this field. An overwhelming amount of documentary data has been readily available since 1945 for research workers. Much that has been produced in the past decade on this subject has been description at a low level, in some cases hardly more than an expanded account of what one could find in the various organizations' yearbooks or the descriptive literature put out by governments concerning these international bodies and their structure and procedure. An abundance of data, an eagerness on the part of publishers to put out simplified accounts of these often seemingly complex organizations, and the pressure to make the most of this market no doubt account for some of the superficial research which has been published. Like the era when diplomatic history lived off the Department of State's *Foreign Relations of the United States* and other convenient compilations of official documents, the past decade has been a heyday for the compile-annotate-clip-and-paste type of research for international organization studies.

Of all the 308 studies in international relations in progress in 1950 which were analyzed by Hawley and Dexter, the studies of the United Nations and other supranational or international organizations made up *one-sixth* of the total. In their analysis of research published in five political science journals, Waldo and Nash found eleven articles on international organization (including international courts) appearing in 1952–54 as against only two such articles in 1939–41.[5] In a very real sense this was a

[5] Only four journals were reviewed for 1939–41. Information taken from MS of Dwight Waldo's study of trends in political science in several countries, prepared for the Social Science Division of Unesco.

revival of research interest in international organization comparable to the level of research interest which the League of Nations had engendered in the period 1920–32, before the League entered upon its eclipse in effectiveness and appeal. A reading of the published lists of doctoral dissertations in political science and in history in progress at American universities for these two periods[6] reveals the high degree of interest in international organization. There were more titles in fact on this aspect of international relations in political science dissertations than on any other single topic. The research interests of doctoral candidates may reflect the research interests of their teachers, and hence serve as an indication of what advanced scholars are studying or believe to be worth studying.

It might be noted that the location of the headquarters of both the United Nations and the Organization of American States in the United States has accentuated the interest of American scholars in international organization research. It is also probably true that American scholars and students probably incline more toward an interest in organization and in an action program than in the study of more abstract legal or theoretical principles unless they relate to specific actionable cases or procedures. We are, or tend to be, preoccupied with what is happening or what has happened, which can be described empirically, measured quantitatively, and evaluated. We like the concrete or solid stuff of international affairs which will not draw us off into undocumented fields of metaphysical speculation and theorizing.[7] Our researchers tend to begin with the aspects of international affairs

6 There are annual lists for political science during 1945–55, but no lists were published in the *American Political Science Review* for 1921, 1923, or 1924. Doctoral dissertation titles in history were published annually by the Division of Historical Research of the Carnegie Institution through 1938, but have appeared since then only as supplements to the *American Historical Review* or as separate publications (1947, 1949, and 1952).

7 See Frederick S. Dunn's admonition regarding the lessons for "greater effectiveness in future research": "The first is the need for sticking closely to *concrete* cases at all stages of research. One should begin with the observation of real events and processes, and never get very far away from them." See "The Present Course of International Relations Research," *World Politics*, II, 94–95.

which are readily observed and measured, and often the research does not go beyond discovering and recording of empirical data.

Beginning in the wartime years (1941–45) and developing rapidly after the war there was a deep interest in United States foreign relations and our foreign policy. Research in this field tended to be principally historical studies, with some analysis and description of current problems.[8] In the main, research in the early postwar years focused on American relations with and policy toward specific countries or world geographic areas. A later emphasis came into this field in the form of studies of the nature of American foreign policy and how the foreign policies of the United States have developed. The postwar publication of a flood of memoirs by persons close to President Franklin D. Roosevelt—ex-government officials, retired military and naval officers, and others—provided a body of material which generously supplemented the emerging volumes of official records and documents. Out of this raw material a researcher could fashion, or easily find, an account of how the government of the United States had come to adopt a particular policy or policies; why it had not adopted possible alternative policies; and often there were estimates of the consequences of these policies, whether in the adopted or the rejected category.

Wartime experience in military or civilian branches of the government exposed many academicians to the *action* problems in international affairs. It was not surprising therefore that the problem approach, which is so much a part of any American's daily view of life and way of living, should become a popular method in studying American foreign policy. It was not really a new method, but the paraphernalia of the problem-paper method was taken up widely, helped along by the substantial propagation of this approach by the Brookings Institution through some fourteen seminars held in different parts of the country for college

8 Such as the series of books edited by former Under Secretary of State Sumner Welles under the general title of "The American Foreign Policy Library," published by Harvard University Press.

and university teachers of international affairs in the period from 1947 to 1952, and through its annual publication *Major Problems of U.S. Foreign Policy,* published from 1947 through 1954.

Problems of relations between the United States and other countries; of American participation in multinational organizations, conferences, or organizations for defense; of American aid to underdeveloped or war-devastated areas, to refugees, and to areas threatened by Communist subversion or aggression; problems of peace making, all took a prominent place in American academic research in the decade 1945–55 even as these same problems dominated the front pages of the newspapers. The similarity of research topics for a high percentage of scholarly research and the headline news has helped to fix in the minds of some academic administrators the idea that the study and teaching of international affairs is really little more than a ponderous rehash of what could be read in more dashing, if less accurate, exposition in the daily press and other periodicals. This belief has been an affliction which has done the scholarly study of international affairs immense harm, but the scholars are partly to blame. Until fairly recently the subjects which they have chosen and the manner in which their research has often been reported and published have helped to confirm this common misconception about the true nature of the study of international affairs.

In the last few years there has been a marked trend toward more basic research, outside the strictly operational research which is being done under various kinds of government contracts or grants-in-aid. In the field of American policy, for example, scholars have begun to do more than just write *about* it in essentially reportorial, descriptive, and editorial terms. They have begun to dig more deeply into the nature of the policy-making and the decision-making process.[9] The role of different interest groups in foreign policy making has been studied increasingly,

---

[9] Twenty-nine studies of political factors in the formation or execution of American foreign policy were identified by Hawley and Dexter in the 308 ongoing studies in international relations. *Op. cit.,* p. 474.

and there has been more and more use of the findings of sociologists and psychologists and their studies as to what motivates leaders, either as individuals or in groups of "elites" or as economic or professional "classes." The anatomy of political forces and the action and interaction of values, habits of thought, traditions, fears, and expectations have come under more careful study for their relationship to the course of international affairs.

There has been a growing interest and increased research in the field of a general theory of international relations. This interest is inspired by a sound desire on the part of scholars in international affairs to make their research more "scientific," to bring to it an aura of respectability among scholars in other fields of study, and also to give it a broader perspective and conceptual framework. Hawley and Dexter reported some twenty-five studies on "the general theory of international relations" out of the 308 they reviewed in the field of international relations.[10] In recent months there have been both books[11] and articles[12] reflecting this concern for the foundation stones, so to speak, of international relations theory and practice. Considerable heat has been generated in the course of a recent "great debate" over morality *versus* power in international politics, and some research efforts among the academicians have been promoted by this debate. There has also been increased study of the particular theories of some of the leading theorists of international relations. Despite this considerable effort, however, it would appear that we still are far from a widely acceptable general theory of international relations.

One of the major branches of research in international affairs since 1945 has been the somewhat ill-defined but closely related field of area studies. Where the research has been on some aspect of a foreign culture, with concentration on only its intrinsic features

---

[10] *Op. cit.*, p. 474.

[11] For example, Feliks Gross, *Foreign Policy Analysis* (New York: Philosophical Library, 1954), Quincy Wright, *The Study of International Relations* (New York: Appleton-Century-Crofts, 1955). See also the writings of Professor Hans J. Morgenthau on the nature of international politics.

[12] For example, Kenneth W. Thompson, "Toward a Theory of International Politics," *American Political Science Review*, XLIX (September 1955), 733–46.

and local significance, it has usually had little applicability to international affairs. If, however, a study deals with aspects of a foreign culture or society that may directly, or indirectly, condition relations with other cultures or societies in another nation-state or that have some direct bearing on the program of an international body, such a study can more readily be classified with other recognizable international affairs research. Area studies have ranged widely from primarily descriptive, fact-finding collections of data[13] to more unified and conceptualized research on social, political, and economic forces in given countries or large geographic areas. The endless extent of possible research in area studies has disheartened some scholars and frustrated others, but the work of building up a body of more accurate and complete knowledge about all areas of the world has gone on quite vigorously in the past decade.

In addition to a long-standing interest in Western Europe by American scholars, the Soviet Union, along with the countries within its sphere of influence, has been the new area most fully studied. The incentives for study of this part of the world have been considerable: mainly the extensive lack of knowledge of the U.S.S.R. coupled with the prominent position of that country in international affairs since the end of World War II. The philanthropic foundations and the government agencies supporting research have been generous in financing studies of the Soviet Union and Eastern Europe, and the availability of considerable Russian material in English translation in the last few years has helped overcome a language deficiency that had previously hampered research on Russia in American colleges and universities.[14] Obstacles of access to the area and to materials on the area, as noted earlier, hamper this research.

---

13 For example, researches for the Human Relations Area Files.

14 A notable aid to research in this field has been the publication of the weekly *Current Digest of the Soviet Press,* for the past eight years, by the Joint Committee on Slavic Studies of the American Council of Learned Societies and the Social Science Research Council. This committee has also been responsible for the translation of many important Russian books.

Latin American studies flourished during World War II, aided by the factor of accessibility, when most other areas of the world were closed or otherwise unattractive to academic researchers, and by generous support from American governmental agencies and foundations. With the end of the war and the reopening of Europe and most of the Far East to American scholars these non-American areas recovered their prewar status in research, and by 1950 they surpassed Latin America in popularity and became second in number only to studies of the Soviet Union and its satellites, while Latin American studies dropped in appeal.

In very recent years there have been a number of efforts to stimulate more research by American academic scholars on geographic areas hitherto largely neglected at our colleges and universities. The Near and Middle East, South Asia, Southeast Asia, and Africa have successively (and in that order) been spotlighted for attention. Watching the foundations and the learned societies scurry from one focus of area studies to another in the last ten years gave one a picture of a sort of slow-motion (but not always slow) Easter-egg hunt. At a distance—from Europe for example—this commotion may have appeared amusing. The purpose was serious, however, and the need was real.[15]

The Social Science Research Council's Committee on World Area Research was established in 1946. This committee sponsored a survey of facilities for teaching and research in area studies at American universities[16] and organized two large conferences on area research and training.[17] The committee also supported a careful analysis of the problems in undertaking a big program

[15] For an account of the facilities for area research as they existed in early 1951 at American colleges and universities, see Wendell C. Bennett, *Area Studies in American Universities* (New York: Social Science Research Council, 1951). This report deals chiefly with about twenty institutions having graduate area programs.

[16] Robert B. Hall, *Area Studies* (New York: Social Science Research Council, 1947), Pamphlet 3.

[17] See Charles Wagley, *Area Research and Training* (New York: Social Science Research Council, 1948), Pamphlet 6; and Richard H. Heindel, "The Present Position of Foreign Area Studies" (Mimeographed; New York: Social Science Research Council, 1950).

to increase our knowledge of other areas of the world. This study by Julian H. Steward became in his words "an inquiry into some possible scientific concepts, theories, and methods for interdisciplinary area research."[18]

The pursuit of area studies was enhanced by foundation grants for individual study in world areas and for group conferences on problems and topics for research in some of the neglected areas. For example, the Committee on the Near and Middle East (established in January 1951) of the Social Science Research Council sponsored a conference at Princeton University in October 1952 for the purpose of "stimulating research and of drawing attention to the growing importance of reliable information about the peoples of the Near East."[19] The members of the committee were (and still are) all academic people and many of the participants at the Princeton conference were from academic institutions. In a somewhat similar effort to stimulate research in a world area largely neglected by researchers, the National Research Council and the Social Science Research Council sponsored a conference on problems of area research in Africa in October 1953. This conference (also held at Princeton) stressed the theme Stability and Change in African Society, and all the papers read at the meeting were the work of academic researchers.[20] Some area research projects were more narrowly focused than might be suggested by the above comments,[21] but the concern in the early 1950's was to fill in gaps of continental or subcontinental dimensions through academic area research in American institutions of higher learning.

From the most recent listings of completed studies in the *Re-*

18 *Area Research: Theory and Practice* (New York: Social Science Research Council, 1950), Bulletin 63.

19 See Bryce Wood, "The Conference on the Near East: Social Dynamics and the Cultural Setting," *SSRC Items*, VII (March 1953), 1–7.

20 See Bryce Wood, "The Conference on Problems of Area Research in Contemporary Africa," *SSRC Items*, VII (December 1953), 42–46.

21 For example, the Modern Chinese History Project of the Far Eastern and Russian Institute of the University of Washington as reported by Franz Michael and Stanley Spector in "Cooperative Area Research," *World Politics*, II (October 1949), 148–55.

search Lists compiled by the External Research Staff of the Department of State it is apparent that a very considerable amount
of academic research has been undertaken in the last few years
in these world areas which were once almost neglected at our
academic centers.[22] Research reported in these very useful periodic
Lists includes some theses for the M.A. and numerous doctoral
dissertations as well as post-doctoral research; thus, there is evidence that the efforts to stimulate research in several world areas
has penetrated below the level of that of advanced scholars, participants at scholarly conferences, and membership of special
committees organized to develop this research.

One big boost to area research for young scholars as well as for
the more advanced scholars has been the Fulbright program for
study abroad (involving some twenty countries) which has generously supplemented the very limited financial resources for
foreign study available prior to 1950. More recently the Smith-
Mundt Act has helped research abroad in areas not included
within the Fulbright exchange program.

In 1952 the Ford Foundation initiated a comprehensive program of fellowships for foreign study and research for young college graduates and for advanced training of specialists. This
splendid program was focused first on Asia and the Near and
Middle East. Later it was expanded to include Eastern Europe
and then to include Africa. These fellowships, for periods of one
to two and one-half years, have made possible foreign field work
and intensive foreign language and other training in the United
States to an unprecedented degree. The hundreds of applications
received yearly by the foundation's Board on Overseas Training
and Research attest to the interest in area studies which has been
stimulated by the obvious need for research and by faculty

---

[22] See *Research Lists* No. 1.5 (U.S.S.R.), No. 3.5 (Southeast Asia), No. 7.5
(Eastern Europe), No. 9.5 (Near East), No. 10.5 (India, Pakistan, Afghanistan,
Nepal, Iran, Iraq), No. 13.5 (Africa), and No. 14.5 (British Commonwealth)—
all covering the period October 1954–October 1955 (Multilithed; Washington:
External Research Staff, Office of Intelligence Research, U. S. Department of
State).

counselors in academic programs. These students have been led on to advanced study by the fortunate prospect of financial support in generous amounts for adequate periods of study.

It is safe to say, however, that without the support of government exchange scholarships and fellowships, the Ford Foundation and other foundation research fellowships for area studies in American universities would likely be much more haphazard, disorganized, and unproductive.

Some other subjects for research have received special attention and support by research councils and the philanthropic foundations in recent years. One such field of study has been the vitally important one of civil-military relations. Prior to World War II military affairs received very little attention by the social scientists. In the wartime years it became increasingly clear that total war not only was all-embracing in its scope but that the problems of civil-military relations could no longer be taken as a temporary and occasional source of administrative difficulty, which would pass when the war ended. With the early postwar emergence of the cold war and the clear prospect of a most uneasy bipolarization of the world for a long time to come, social scientists began to take stock of what was known and what was not known about the problems of civil-military relations.

In June 1952 the Social Science Research Council established a Committee on Civil-Military Relations Research, later renamed the Committee on National Security Policy Research. The committee's concern was "in research bearing upon those problems of public policy which were posed by the prospect of a continuing high mobilization even in peacetime, and by the continuing necessity for a careful coordination of military, diplomatic, and industrialization policy."[23] This committee developed plans for a program of research grants to individuals for studies in the history of American military policy beginning in the autumn of

[23] See William T. R. Fox, "Civil-Military Relations Research," *World Politics,* VI (January 1954), 278–88. See also *Civil-Military Relations: An Annotated Bibliography, 1940–1952* (New York: Columbia University Press, 1954).

1954.[24] Under this program several research grants have been made, and work has gone forward where otherwise it would likely have lagged. Other sources of aid have come forward since 1954, and it is reasonable to expect that research well started in this field will go forward and be increased.[25] Those teachers who have tended to be very idealistic and hence have shut their eyes to war and its concomitants need to be much more active in researching and teaching this aspect of international affairs. Woefully weak are academic library collections of journals and books which report the developments in military tactics and science, and the thinking of leading military officers and their research staffs. Military affairs, however much we might wish them to be only an unhappy aberration, may be in fact a permanent aspect of our lives. Indeed, modern war may no longer be only a matter of politics carried on in another form, but a genuinely new and horrible feature of present and future daily human affairs. The research scholars in the social sciences and the civilian and military practitioners in government must cooperate more fully to help each other cope with new problems of theory and of practice in the role of warfare in modern society.

What areas or topics in international affairs particularly need research now?

Looking out on the broad, sprawling field of international affairs research, one is simultaneously impressed by the wide

[24] See Gordon A. Craig and Bryce Wood, "The History of American Military Policy: A New Program of Grants for Research," *SSRC Items,* VIII (June 1954), 13–15, and X (June 1954), 17–18, on new grants. See also Bryce Wood, "Report on the Conference on National Security Policy: Problems of Research and Teaching," *SSRC Items,* XI (September 1957), 29–32.

[25] Notably a Twentieth Century Fund grant for a research program in civil-military relations as they affect the making of national policy. Dr. Harold Stein is directing this three-year project at Princeton. The Carnegie Corporation also made a grant for a research program on the education of military officers who participate or may be expected to participate in formulating national policies; Professors John W. Masland and Lawrence I. Radway have carried on this study at Dartmouth College. The Institute of War and Peace Studies at Columbia University, under the direction of Professor William T. R. Fox, has been another center for studies in civil-military relations in recent years.

range of subjects and the quantity of research now going on, and yet one is appalled by the vast amount of research which needs to be done. If international affairs research is to become a truly scientific enterprise, much must be done to increase the store of knowledge, to make more of this knowledge useful to mankind, and to open avenues to future research that will be scientific, meaningful, and useful. Perhaps this question of what needs to be done can best be approached by setting up some categories for research efforts. Three such categories may be established as possibly useful markers on the vast plain of work to be done.

1. *What is there to be known about past and present international affairs?* This is the broadest and most basic category for research; in a sense this is its most scientific foundation. An unlimited amount of research could be undertaken in this area and a considerable amount of what has already been done—or is now going on—comes under this rubric. The research in this category will be largely historical, empirical, and legal studies. It will deal with definitions and descriptions of the participants in international affairs; the acts and failures to act by the participants; the alternatives which faced given participants at given times and on given problems in international affairs; the significance of factors of natural environment, population, and strategic locations; the nature of national power; the role of ideologies and the steadily changing concepts of national interest for each participant in international affairs; and so on. This field of research will be concerned with the nature of international affairs and the whole spectrum of *why* and *how* and *to what end* international relations take place.

The whole range of human affairs is related to this field of research in international affairs, because individual behavior and motivations may be as important to analyze and understand as group behavior and motivation. In fact, the observed actions and apparent motivations of "social" animals and even some insects may provide some clues to human actions and motivations under comparable stresses of hunger, fear, urge to self-preservation, desire for prestige, and other basic attributes of life in groups or herds or "colonies." Out of this research will come ideas and broad theories useful to the understanding of international relations. Scholars devoted to the study of international affairs will not likely do this research, but they will need to draw on the work of others who have researched these fields.

No science has ever had all the time and support needed to define it and to organize its knowledge before it was put to pragmatic tests and demands. No science in fact is yet complete, for knowledge is an endless frontier in time and space and comprehension. Inevitably there are pressures to limit the scope of research in any science, and the workers in any science must be prepared for these pressures by those who ask *"what* knowledge for *what* purpose?" and who are impatient with those who seek just *any* increase of knowledge in their field regardless of its present or possible utility. The second field of research in international affairs might therefore be stated as:

2. *What do we need to know about international affairs?* This might, in fact, in the context of this report, be narrowed to what do Americans need to know about international affairs which could conceivably be discovered or elaborated on by researchers at American colleges and universities?

This second category of research is primarily the domain of "operational" and obviously "usable" research. It is this category of research which government agencies have largely supported, although there are a few exceptions for general studies of the nature of international affairs. Most of the thousands of researchers in the government who are engaged in intelligence work are busily doing this kind of research. Research in this category lends itself to government organization and close administration, for the "targets" can be more clearly defined and the timing can be set, if not actually oppressively prescribed. There are broader topics of research within this category but they still are of essentially the operational type, such as how to determine the effectiveness of a given propaganda or information program; how to appeal to, or influence, a particular foreign political elite; or how to harmonize a particular controversy between two nations with justice and equity. Broader studies may be directed to the relationship of an arms race to the chances of war on the part of the rivals in that race; or to the factors requisite to group solidarity and consensus for action on controversial public problems; or the social and political consequences of sudden economic development in underdeveloped areas; or the significance in social and political terms of new scientific discoveries and technological developments. These are all examples of appropriate topics for research which come in the "need to know" category.

3. *Research which is highly value-motivated in purpose and objectives* is a third category for research in international affairs. This is the category in which one finds studies directed to the specific question of the preservation of peace;[26] or to the prevention of war; or to the advancement of free trade among nations; or to the advancement of human rights for all, or a certain group, of the world's people; or the strengthening of the United Nations; and the like. There are in these and similar studies a number of implicit qualifications to the research project, and there tends to be an emotional commitment on the part of the researcher to find data and arguments to serve and support a particular objective in international affairs.

In the first category of research mentioned (what is to be known about international affairs), the sound researcher is interested in all pertinent facts—let the chips fall where they may —as he is intent only on cutting a path or paths through the forest of the facts or the unproven concepts about international affairs. In the second category (what do we need to know about

[26] The Institute for Social Research in Oslo, Norway, offered a prize in 1951 for the best paper on the problem of the relevance of research to the problems of peace. See Institute for Social Research [Oslo], *Research for Peace* (Amsterdam: North-Holland Publishing Co., 1954) for an account of this contest and the text of the prize-winning essays by Quincy Wright, W. F. Cottrell, and Ch. Boasson, with a review of the contest contributions by Ingemund Gullvag.

international affairs), the researcher is concentrating on certain specific trees or groups of trees in the forest of knowledge and chops on them for a specific (usually "operational") purpose. In the third category, following this metaphor, the researcher works in the forest of knowledge to chop down certain trees to help build a particular edifice or institution on which he and others have set a high value goal.

The worker in the third field tends to be more on the defensive about what he is doing and particularly about what he has done if it later turns out that the goal he helped to serve or hoped to serve is not realized. Certainly much of the academic research in international affairs after World War I had this value-directed quality, and the researchers often became emotionally committed to what they were studying—for example, the League of Nations, pacific settlement of disputes by arbitration, disarmament, the idea of national self-determination and mandates for non-self-governing peoples. When much of what they hoped for, and had done research to help develop, did not live up to their and others' expectations, they were often disillusioned and sometimes embittered.[27] Their reactions often served to discourage others from doing research on the same subjects even without the same motivations. Idealism is good, and it is found in substantial measure in most teachers and scholars; the need is for preserving objectivity along with idealism.

Value-directed research may also include research which has as its purpose proving that a particular individual, group, class, or nation was the cause of certain actions (such as war, racial or religious discrimination, or destructive economic nationalism), actions that are generally deplored in principle by citizens in many countries who stress morality as the basis of proper action in international affairs, although their daily lives may not be so governed. This is research to find and fix guilt or malfeasance

---

[27] See William T. R. Fox, "Interwar International Relations Research: The American Experience," *World Politics*, II (October 1949), 67–70, for comments on the value-directed research after World War I.

which brought about damage to values deeply cherished, at least in the abstract. Research to "prove" war guilt is perhaps most conspicuous in this category, but other comparable researches of the past decade will come to the minds of students of international affairs.

Where should the efforts of researchers and the financial resources and facilities of academic institutions, the philanthropic foundations, and the government be directed in international affairs? If we cannot cover all three categories described above— and we obviously cannot, even under optimum conditions, in the next decade—where should the emphasis be? What should the priorities be?

Conclusion

The clearest need in international affairs research would seem to be in the category of understanding the phenomenon itself. What is the nature of the relations we call international; how much is at the level of governments of nation-states; how much is at the level of peoples; how much is at the level of individuals in relation to other individuals? Is it possible to de-emotionalize study in international relations so that the researcher observes the facts in the same way that a physicist watches the fissioning of matter, or the effects of wind currents on objects in a wind tunnel, or the emergence, consequences, and disappearance of sunspots? From historical records and by contemporary observation and deduction we must learn more of the nature of international relations and of the extent to which actions in this field may be measured, reliably projected forward, and predicted dependably. Unless researchers in international relations can formulate more scientific qualities and concepts of international affairs, they will have to reconcile themselves to being regarded as little better than chroniclers who can recount events but cannot explain them convincingly, or sooth-sayers who blindly speculate on the future.

Research must be increased in the second category (needs)

with particular attention to studies on how groups organize, act, and disintegrate; on the qualities and characteristics of leadership by individuals and by elites; on the requirements for the adequate communication of ideas and information from one individual to another and from one group to another; on the relationship of developments in the natural sciences and in engineering to the problems of the organization and management of societies and nations; on the political processes of policy making and decision making; on the problems of the management of governmental institutions subjected to the pressures of professional, military, economic, and other special-interest groups; on the capacity of individuals to adjust wisely to constantly rising standards of living and to rising expectations for still higher standards of living; and the meaning of developments in war-making potential which can utterly destroy our accumulated wealth, comfort, and security with cataclysmic suddenness.

Despite the omnipresent fact of potential doom for civilization through the reckless use of weapons already available—to say nothing of what may soon be invented—it seems that value-directed research focused on preserving peace and preventing war will be less than effective (and hence ought to have a lower priority) until the basic elements of international affairs and human conduct have been more adequately explored. If—as may prove to be the case—the research findings of scholars in many fields show that men act in irrational ways despite their vast knowledge and the innumerable exhortations for better, wiser, and more moral action, then studies on preserving peace would be superfluous anyway. If the fog of emotional seeking for peace could be lifted and we could see whatever is to be revealed in the clear, cold light of scientific inquiry, we might then better achieve what we want than if we proceed from a basis of what we wish to find.

There is some reason to expect that research in international affairs in the future will be less value-directed and more scientific than it has been. Foundations supporting international affairs research now put less emphasis on the overt search for peace (or "the speedy abolition of international war between the so-called civilized nations" as Andrew Carnegie charged the trustees of the Carnegie Peace Fund in his letter to them of December 14, 1910) and put more emphasis on the general problem of human behavior and the nature and management of the institutions which mankind has developed to advance, regulate, and control human behavior.

If the sources of financial and other support for research in international affairs become more objective and more dispassionate in their approach to international affairs, and if the scholars can match this with their own increased objectivity and personal detachment from the stuff of their research, there is some reason to believe that a science of international affairs can be developed and that it will not be at a disadvantage in "scientificness" when it confronts the natural sciences and the discoveries of the latter which have changed and are changing man and the world in which man lives. This is a great endeavor in which academic researchers ought to play an important role. It will require bold action by administrators to find the financial means to provide the support which scholars will need to do their work. Scholars will have to be bold and energetic. The objectives to be served are of the highest order, and we can only hope that out of the scholars' researches will come the concepts and the *modus operandi* for a truly "new" world; free, orderly, and satisfying for mankind.

Appendix: Notes from Some Institutional Self-Survey Reports*

For Chapter 1

Some cooperative as well as individual research programs are offered at Fisk University, through the Department of Social Sciences. ("Report on Fisk University and World Affairs," Document No. 74 [Feb. 1, 1955], p. 8.)

"In the international field, the [New York University] faculty has published a total of 40 books and 186 articles in this span of five years [from 1948 to 1953]. Ph.D. dissertations number 50." For a table showing the spread of research in world affairs and suggested plans for the study of international relations, see "New York University in World Affairs" (Document No. 23 [Sept. 15, 1953], p. 15).

Factors operating to prevent the maximum use of scholarship and fellowship funds—financial considerations and distribution of workload—are discussed in "The State University of Iowa and World Affairs" (Document No. 80 [May 15, 1955], p. 102).

See also "University of Alabama in World Affairs," Document No. 70 [Dec. 15, 1954], p. 45.

"Despite the lack of any special encouragement a small number of faculty members [at the University of Alabama] have been actively engaged in research in international problems. The postcard poll, which brought responses from 334 faculty, indicated nine members of the social science department actively working in this field. Four were in political science, three in economics, and two in history. Most of the studies were political or economic rather than cultural, social or ethnic. . . . Of 166 books published by members of the faculty during the past five years, only seven, or about 4 percent, dealt with international affairs. Of the 1,744 articles, 33, or less than 2 percent, were in this field. From a total of 634 master's theses, only 18, or about 3 percent, dealt

---

* The reports of institutions on their self-surveys of activities and resources bearing on international relations, from which the following excerpts and summaries are taken, were published in mimeographed form by the Carnegie Endowment for International Peace under the title *Universities and World Affairs*. For each note the title of the report from which the material is taken, document number, date of publication, and page reference are given.

with international problems." ("University of Alabama in World Affairs," Document No. 70 [Dec. 15, 1954], p. 44.)

For faculty interest in foreign affairs, see "Wayne University and World Affairs" (Document No. 55 [Sept. 15, 1954], p. 4); "The Role of the University of Oregon in World Affairs" (Document No. 61 [Nov. 1, 1954], p. 36); and "The University of North Dakota in World Affairs" (Document No. 80 [May 15, 1955], pp. 98–99).

For recommendations regarding the investigation of research bearing on world affairs, see "The State University of Iowa and World Affairs" (Document No. 80 [May 15, 1955], pp. 98-99).

For research facilities available to the special student, see "Michigan State College and World Affairs" (Document No. 69 [Dec. 15, 1956], p. 13).

At Goucher College no special provision is made, but there is a willingness to arrange for sabbaticals and reduce the teaching load for those engaged in concentrated research. ("Goucher College in World Affairs," Document No. 59 [Oct. 1, 1954], p. 19.)

For Chapter 2

That financial problems are paramount in university research is shown in "The University of Washington in World Affairs" (Document No. 25 [1953], p. 10): "The initiative in much of the basic research resides outside the university in the hands of the federal government which supplies the funds for most of the university projects. A problem of orienting basic research plans to the provisions of government contracts stems from the financial inability of the various university faculties to support adequately their own projects with necessary research materials and equipment."

Special provision is made for leave to study abroad and this will encourage staff members in extending research. ("Central Missouri State College in World Affairs," Document No. 76 [Feb. 1, 1955], p. 5.)

Reporting on research studies on world affairs at the State College of Washington, the World Affairs Survey Committee found that ". . . aside from some incalculable contributions to research in world affairs and international relations, such as additions to library, reduction in teaching load for staff engaged in such research, etc., an extremely small portion of the institution's total funds are devoted to the direct support of such research." ("Final Report of the World Affairs Survey Committee, State College of Washington," Document No. 27 [Oct. 28, 1953], p. 27.)

"The University of Florida provides funds for some research material and books, some research assistants, and typing, but makes no provision for organized research in international relations as such, aside from the work of the School of Inter-American Studies. It does encourage general research in international relations as part of the over-all University research program." ("A Survey of the University of Florida and World Affairs," Document No. 78 [April 15, 1955], p. 21.) See also the "Final Report of the World Affairs Survey Committee, State College of Washington" (Document No. 27 [Oct. 28, 1953], p. 28).

For recent improvements in local research facilities, see "The Role of the University of Oregon in World Affairs" (Document No. 61 [Nov. 1, 1954], p. 23).

Cooperative research supports a close relationship between research and training, as is shown in "The University of Washington in World Affairs," (Document No. 25 [1953], p. 5).

Regarding the possibility of establishing a Latin-American Affairs Institute at the Texas Christian University, see "Texas Christian University in International Affairs" (Document No. 34 [Feb. 1, 1954], p. 16).

Recommendations for establishing an Institute of Public Affairs at the University of Michigan, "The Function and Scope of International Affairs at the University of Michigan" (p. 14).

For Chapter 6

Area specialization in Far Eastern and Russian studies for the M.A. and Ph.D. candidates in political science, history, and economics at the University of Washington is discussed in "The University of Washington in World Affairs" (Document No. 25 [Oct. 23, 1953], p. 5).

A partial list of theses and dissertations in international relations in the last four years, i.e., 1951–55, at the University of Florida can be found in "A Survey of the University of Florida and World Affairs" (Document No. 78 [April 15, 1955], p. 26).

The World Affairs Survey Committee at the State College of Washington pointed out the need for research in world economics, propaganda and information, area studies, technical assistance, human relations and understanding, health, education, and semantics. ("Final Report of the World Affairs Survey Committee, State College of Washington," Document No. 27 [Oct. 28, 1953], p. 29. See also the report of the same committee for June 1953, Appendix C.)

For a list of subjects investigated by faculty members at Wellesley College, see "Wellesley Report" (Document No. 8 [Oct. 22, 1952], pp. 25 and 26).

For some topics in world affairs chosen for doctoral dissertations, see "The Function and Scope of International Affairs at the University of Michigan," p. 10.

For some examples of typical topics for research among candidates for the M.A. degree, see "Texas Christian University in International Affairs" (Document No. 36 [Feb. 1, 1956], p. 7); and "Agnes Scott College and World Affairs" (Document No. 47 [Sept. 15, 1954], p. 2).

Bibliography: Suggestions for Further Reading

ALMOND, GABRIEL A. *The American People and Foreign Policy.* New York: Harcourt, Brace & Co., 1950. The stages of analysis used by Dr. Almond in this significant study of American public opinion are described on pp. 8–10; some very useful bibliographic notes on writings in this field appear on pp. 245–58.

———. "The Politics of German Business," reprint from *World Politics,* VIII (January 1956), 157–86.

AMERICAN COUNCIL OF LEARNED SOCIETIES. *A Program for Near Eastern Studies in the United States.* Report of the Committee on Near Eastern Studies. Washington: The Council, 1949.

——— AND SOCIAL SCIENCE RESEARCH COUNCIL, JOINT COMMITTEE ON SOUTHERN ASIA. *Southern Asia Studies in the United States: A Survey and a Plan.* Philadelphia, Pa.: University of Pennsylvania, 1951. A thorough case study of an area approach to research.

AMERICAN COUNCIL ON EDUCATION, COMMITTEE ON INSTITUTIONAL RE-SEARCH POLICY. *Sponsored Research Policy of Colleges and Universities.* Washington: The Council, 1954.

AMERICAN POLITICAL SCIENCE ASSOCIATION. *Goals for Political Science, 1951: Report of the Committee for the Advancement of Teaching.* New York: Dryden Press, 1951.

American Political Science Review. (Now published quarterly.) Very useful for information on new research projects, programs, and institutes as reported in the "News and Notes" section of each issue and in occasional special articles; for example:

a) "Research in Comparative Politics," a seminar report jointly prepared by Roy Macridis and Richard Cot; and "Comments on the Seminar Report," by Carl J. Friedrich, Harold D. Lasswell, Herbert A. Simon, Ralph J. D. Braibanti, G. Lowell Field, and Dwight Waldo. *American Political Science Review,* XLVII, September 1953.

b) "Princeton's Foreign Policy Analysis Project," *American Political Science Review,* XLVII (June 1953), 610.

ANDREWS, F. EMERSON. *Philanthropic Foundations.* New York: Russell Sage Foundation, 1956. The most recent study of the programs and policies of the American foundations.

BAILEY, STEPHEN K., AND OTHERS. *Research Frontiers in Politics and Government.* Brookings Institution Lectures—1955. Washington: The Institution, 1955.

BENNETT, WENDELL CLARK. *Area Studies in American Universities.* New York: Social Science Research Council, 1951.

BENSON, O. *Toward a New Eclecticism in International Studies.* A report stemming from the Curriculum Study Project, Department of

Political Science, Northwestern University. March 1955. Mimeographed. Evanston, Ill.: The Department, Northwestern University.

BERGSON, ABRAM. "The Conference on Soviet Economic Growth: Conditions and Perspectives," *SSRC Items*, September 1952.

BLEGEN, THEODORE C., AND COOPER, RUSSELL M. (eds.). *The Preparation of College Teachers*. Washington: American Council on Education, 1950.

BROOKINGS INSTITUTION, INTERNATIONAL STUDIES STAFF. *Report on a Conference on the Teaching of International Relations, Charlottesville, Virginia, January 26–28, 1950*. Washington: The Institution, 1950.

Bulletin of the Research Exchange on the Prevention of War, Vol. I, No. 1, and issues subsequent to November 1952.

CARNEGIE ENDOWMENT FOR INTERNATIONAL PEACE. *Current Research in International Affairs*. New York: The Endowment, 1952. A selected bibliography of work in progress by private research agencies in the British Commonwealth and the U.S.A., with introductory essay by Frederick S. Dunn.

————. *Institutes of International Affairs*. New York: The Endowment, 1953. Brief notes on private institutes in the United States and Canada which have research and educational programs in international affairs in which many academic scholars participate.

CARTWRIGHT, DARWIN. "The Strategy of Research on International Conferences," *International Social Science Bulletin* (Unesco), Vol. V (1953), No. 2.

CAVERS, DAVID F. "The Developing Field of International Legal Studies," *American Political Science Review*, XLVII (December 1953), 1058–75.

COHEN, O. "The Application of Social Research to Intergroup Relations," *Social Problems*, July 1954, pp. 20–25.

COMMISSION ON THE ORGANIZATION OF THE EXECUTIVE BRANCH OF THE GOVERNMENT [Hoover Commission]. *Intelligence Activities*. A Report to the Congress, June 1955. Washington: Government Printing Office. A report on the "intelligence community" in the American government.

COWAN, L. GRAY. *A History of the School of International Affairs and Associated Area Institutes, Columbia University*. New York: Columbia University Press, 1954.

DAVISON, W. P. "The Role of Mass Communications During the Berlin Blockade." Research memorandum. Hectographed. Santa Monica, Calif.: Rand Corp., 1955.

————. "Some Observations on the Role of Research in Political Warfare." Research memorandum. Hectographed. Santa Monica, Calif.: Rand Corp., 1951.

DEUTSCH, KARL W. *Political Community at the International Level:*

Problem of Definition and Measurement. Princeton University, Organizational Behavior Section, Foreign Policy Analysis Project, Publication No. 2. Princeton, N.J.: The Section, 1953.

DUNN, FREDERICK S. "The Present Course of International Relations Research," *World Politics,* II (October 1949), 80–95. A very good account of the shifting focus of concentration of research interests in international affairs in the war and postwar years.

————. "The Scope of International Relations," *World Politics,* I (October 1948), 142–46.

FLACK, MICHAEL J. "The Field and Study of International Relations: A Bibliography for *The Teaching of International Politics* ed. Vernon Van Dyke." Mimeographed. Iowa City, Iowa: Department of Political Science, State University of Iowa, December 1955.

FOX, WILLIAM T. R. "Civil-Military Relations Research: The SSRC Committee and Its Research Survey," *World Politics,* VI (January 1954), 278–88.

————. "Inter-War International Relations Research: The American Experience," *World Politics,* II (October 1949), 67–79. A very useful summary account of major research trends and achievements in the period between World War I and World War II.

FURNISS, EDGAR S., JR. *The Office of the Premier in French Foreign Policy-Making: An Application of Decision-Making Analysis.* Princeton University, Organizational Behavior Section, Foreign Policy Analysis Series No. 5. Princeton, N.J.: The Section, 1954. A demonstration of a method of research and analysis applied to a particular problem.

GEE, WILSON. *Research Barriers in the South.* New York: Century Co., 1932. Answers to a questionnaire on the affect of salaries, cost of living, teaching load, etc., on the quantity and quality of academic research.

GEORGE, ALEXANDER L. "Prediction of Political Action by Means of Propaganda Analysis." Research memorandum. Hectographed. Santa Monica, Calif.: Rand Corp., 1955.

GOOD, C. V. AND SCOTES, D. E. *Methods of Research.* New York: Appleton-Century-Crofts, 1954.

GOODWIN, GEOFFREY, L. (ed.). *The University Teaching of International Relations.* International Studies Conference. New York: Macmillan Co., 1951.

GRAHAM, MILTON D. *Federal Utilization of Social Science Research: Exploration of the Problems.* Washington: Brookings Institution, 1954. A very good review of the extent of federally supported social science research and congressional attitudes regarding government grants for such research and the failure of the National Science Foundation program to include social sciences.

GROSS, FELIKS. *Foreign Policy Analysis*. New York: Philosophical Library, 1954.

GUETZKOW, HAROLD. "Long-Range Research in International Relations," *American Perspective*, Fall 1950, pp. 421–40.

————. *Multiple Loyalties: Theoretical Approach to a Problem in International Organization*. Center for Research in World Political Institutions, Princeton University, Publication No. 4, Princeton, N.J.: Princeton University Press, 1955.

————. "Researchable Propositions about the Role of Multiple Loyalties in International Affairs." Mimeographed. February 1956. Obtainable from the author of the Graduate School of Industrial Administration, Carnegie Institute of Technology, Pittsburgh, Pa.

GURIAN, WALDEMAR. "On the Study of International Relations," *Review of Politics*, VIII, October 1946.

HALL, ROBERT B. *Area Studies: With Special Reference to Their Implications for Research in the Social Sciences*. New York: Social Science Research Council, May 1947.

"Harvard University Committee on Research in the Social Sciences," *International Social Science Bulletin* (Unesco), V (1953), 419.

HARVARD UNIVERSITY, RUSSIAN RESEARCH CENTER. *Five-Year Report and Current Projects*. Cambridge, Mass.: The Center, May 1953. See also subsequent reports of this active research center.

HAWLEY, C. E., AND DEXTER, L. A. "Recent Political Science Research in American Universities," *American Political Science Review*, XLVI (June 1952), 470–85.

HILSMAN, ROGER, JR. "Intelligence and Policy-Making in Foreign Affairs," *World Politics*, V (October 1952), 9–11.

"The Inter-Departmental Seminar on Technological Change and Social Adjustment, University of Pennsylvania," *International Social Science Bulletin* (Unesco), Vol. IV, No. 2.

KAHIN, GEORGE McT., AND OTHERS. "Committee on Comparative Politics, Social Science Research Council." Reprint from *American Political Science Review*, XLIX (December 1955), 1022–49.

KALIJARVI, TH. V. "International Relations," in E. S. Griffith (ed.), *Research in Political Science*. Chapel Hill: University of North Carolina Press, 1948.

KANTOR, HARRY. *A Bibliography of Unpublished Doctoral Dissertations and Master's Theses Dealing with the Governments, Politics and International Relations of Latin America*. Series 1, Vol. 13. Gainesville, Fla.: Inter-American Bibliographical and Library Association. 1953.

KECSKEMETI, PAUL. "The 'Policy Sciences': Aspiration and Outlook." Reprint from *World Politics*, IV (July 1952), 520–35.

————. "Totalitarian Communications as a Means of Control: A

Note on the Sociology of Propaganda." Research memorandum. Hectographed. Santa Monica, Calif.: RAND Corp., 1950.

KELMAN, H. C. (ed.). "Research Approaches to the Study of War and Peace," *Journal of Social Issues,* 1955, pp. 1-56.

KIRK, GRAYSON L. *The Study of International Relations in American Colleges and Universities.* New York: Council on Foreign Relations, 1947. A report and summary evaluation of a series of conferences held in different parts of the United States in 1946 under the auspices of the Council on Foreign Relations. Many of the issues and problems discussed ten years ago are still vital.

KEY, V. O., JR. "Strategies in Research on Public Affairs," *SSRC Items,* X (September 1956), 29–32.

KLINEBERG, OTTO. *Tensions Affecting International Understanding, A Survey of Research.* New York: Social Science Research Council, 1950.

——. "The Unesco Project on International Tensions," *International Social Science Bulletin* (Unesco), Vol. I (1949), No. 1-2.

KNORR, KLAUS. "Economics and International Relations: A Problem in Teaching," *Political Science Quarterly,* LXII, December 1947.

——. "Foreign Aid as an Instrument of Foreign Policy." Revised. Mimeographed. Princeton, N.J.: Princeton University.

LACY, DAN. "Federal Research Contracts," *American Law Association Bulletin,* July–August 1951.

LERNER, DANIEL, AND LASSWELL, HAROLD D. (eds.). *The Policy Sciences: Recent Developments in Scope and Method.* Stanford, Calif.: Stanford University Press, 1951.

LINEBARGER, G. C., AND ASSOCIATES. *Washington Sources on International Affairs.* College Park, Md.: University of Maryland, Bureau of Public Administration, 1951.

LOWRY, H. AND TAEUSCH, W. *Research, Creative Activity and Thinking.* New York: Carnegie Foundation for the Advancement of Teaching, 1953. A report of a five-year experiment to improve undergraduate teaching through encouragement to research and creative activity by teachers in colleges and universities.

MANNING, C. A. W. (Rapporteur). "General Report on the Teaching of International Relations," Unesco—Experts' Meeting, September 16–19, 1952. [Paris ?]: Unesco's S. S. Conf. 6.1, August 1952.

MASSACHUSETTS INSTITUTE OF TECHNOLOGY. *Research in International Communication: An Advisory Report of the Planning Committee of the Center for International Studies, MIT.* Cambridge, Mass.: Massachusetts Institute of Technology, 1953.

——. Center for International Studies. "The Center for International Studies: A Description." Cambridge, Mass.: Massachusetts Institute of Technology, July 1955. 60 pp. A good account of the organization program, and staff of this productive research center.

MICHAEL, F., AND SPECTOR, S. "Cooperative Area Research," *World Politics*, II (October 1949), 148–55.

MORGENTHAU, HANS J. "Reflections on the State of Political Science," *Review of Politics*, XVII (October 1955), 431–60. A very provocative analysis and discussion of the methods and problems of political science research and study.

MURDOCK, G. P. "The Conceptual Basis of Area Research," *World Politics*, II (July 1950), 571–78.

"A Plan for Research in International Communication: A Report." Reprint from *World Politics*, VI (April 1954), 358–77.

PLISCHKE, ELMER. *American Foreign Relations: A Bibliography of Official Sources*. College Park, Md.: Bureau of Governmental Research, University of Maryland, 1955.

PRESIDENT'S COMMISSION ON HIGHER EDUCATION. *Higher Education for American Democracy*, Vol. I: *Establishing the Goals*. New York: Harper & Bros., 1947.

——. *Higher Education for American Democracy*, Vol. V: *Financing Higher Education*. New York: Harper & Bros., 1947.

"The Research Center on Economic Development and Cultural Change of the University of Chicago," *International Social Science Bulletin* (Unesco), IV, No. 2.

Research for Peace. Essays by Q. Wright, W. F. Cottrell, and Ch. Boasson. Results of a prize contest organized by the Institute for Social Research in Oslo. Amsterdam: North-Holland Publishing Company, 1954.

RICH, S. GROVER, JR. "University Training in International Relations," *Association of American Colleges Bulletin*, XXXIV (December 1953), 598–610.

ROSENBURG, HERBERT H., AND HUBBERT, ERIN. *Opportunities for Federally Sponsored Social Science Research*. Syracuse, N.Y.: Syracuse University, 1951.

RUML, BEARDSLEY, AND TICKTON, SIDNEY G. *Teachers Salaries: Then and Now* (New York: Fund for the Advancement of Education, 1955).

RUSSELL SAGE FOUNDATION. *Effective Use of Social Science Research in the Federal Services*. New York: The Foundation, 1950.

RUSTOW, DANKWART A. *Some Problems of Research in the Politics of Non-Western Countries (With Particular Reference to the Near East)*. A memorandum submitted to the Fourth Meeting of the Committee on Research in Comparative Politics of the Social Science Research Council, Jan. 14, 1955.

SAPIN, B.; SNYDER, R. C.; AND BRUCK, H. W. *An Appropriate Role for the Military in American Foreign Policy-Making: A Research Note*. Princeton University, Organizational Behavior Section, Foreign Policy Analysis Series No. 4. Princeton, N.J.: The Section, 1954.

SAVORD, RUTH. *American Agencies Interested in International Affairs.* New York: Council on Foreign Relations, 1948.

SIBLEY, ELBRIDGE. "The Recruitment, Selection and Training of Social Scientists," *SSRC Bulletin,* Vol. LVIII, 1948. Training and research: pp. 4, 5, 97–100, 102–3, 133–35.

————. *Support for Independent Scholarship and Research.* New York: Social Science Research Council, 1951. Responses by some 1,300 academic scholars and several learned societies and councils on questions relating to problems of financial support and time for research in colleges and universities.

SNYDER, R. C.; BRUCK, H. W.; AND SAPIN, B. *Decision-Making as an Approach to the Study of International Politics.* Princeton University, Organizational Behavior Section, Foreign Policy Analysis Series No. 3, Princeton, N.J.: The Section, 1954.

SOCIAL SCIENCE RESEARCH COUNCIL, COMMITTEE ON ORGANIZATION FOR RESEARCH. *A Directory of Social Science Research Organizations in Universities and Colleges.* New York: The Council, 1950.

SSRC Items. A quarterly published by the Social Science Research Council, New York. Contains very useful information on work of the Council and significant research conferences and occasional other announcements of interest to social scientists.

STEWARD, JULIAN H. *Area Research: Theory and Practice.* New York: Social Science Research Council, 1950.

"The Strategy of Research on International Conferences," *International Social Science Bulletin* (Unesco), V (1953), 278.

Survey of Research and Investigations in Progress and Contemplated in the Field of Latin-American Studies in Colleges and Universities in the U.S. and Canada during the School Year 1952–53. Gainesville, Fla.: School of Inter-American Studies, University of Florida, August 1953.

SUTTON, F. X. *Social Theory and Comparative Politics.* New York: Social Science Research Council, 1955. Prepared for a conference under the auspices of the Committee on Comparative Politics of the SSRC, June 1955.

The Teaching of the Social Sciences in the United States. Paris: Unesco, 1954. Contains a chapter on "The Teaching of International Relations."

THOMPSON, KENNETH. "The Study of International Politics," *Review of Politics,* No. 4, XIV (October 1952), 433–67.

TUVE, MERLE A. "Technology and National Research Policy." Mimeographed. Charlottesville, Va.: Institute of Public Affairs, University of Virginia, July 1953.

UNIVERSITY OF WASHINGTON. *Report on Research* [general] *1953.* Seattle: The University. Includes "Studies in the Far East."

U.S. DEPARTMENT OF STATE, OFFICE OF INTELLIGENCE RESEARCH, EX-

TERNAL RESEARCH STAFF. *Abstracts of Completed Doctoral Dissertations for the Academic Year 1950–1951.* Abstract Series No. 1, March 1952, and subsequent issues.

————. *Southeast Asia.* ERS List No. 3.5, October 1954–October 1955. Formerly External Research Reports, External Research Staff, Office of Intelligence Research, Department of State. The External Research Staff has prepared several such reports; this is cited as an example.

————. *Suggested Topics for Research on Southeast Asia.* April 1953. The External Research Staff has prepared several such lists of suggested topics for research on various areas of the world; this one is cited as an example.

VAN WAGENEN, RICHARD W. *Research in the International Organization Field: Some Notes on a Possible Focus.* Center for Research on World Political Institutions. Princeton, N.J.: Princeton University Press, 1952. 76 pp.

WAGLEY, CHARLES. *Area Research and Training: A Conference Report on the Study of World Areas.* Pamphlet 6. New York: Social Science Research Council, June 1948.

WATERMAN, ALAN T. "Government Support of Research," *Science,* Vol. CX, 1949.

WILSON, HOWARD E. *Universities and World Affairs.* New York: Carnegie Endowment for International Peace, 1951.

WITTFOGEL, KARL. "Russia and Asia: Problems of Contemporary Area Studies and International Relations," *World Politics,* II (July 1950), 445–63.

WRIGHT, QUINCY. "An Analytical Approach to the Subject of World Politics in Teaching and Research," *American Political Science Review,* XXI, 396. Report of a round table at the 1926 meeting of the American Political Science Association.

————. "Method in the Study of War," *World Politics,* I (January 1949), 242–56.

————. *The Study of International Relations.* New York: Appleton-Century-Crofts, 1955. The most comprehensive and ambitious attempt to describe the field of "international relations" and its "subdisciplines" and supporting disciplines.

NOTE: In addition to the reading suggested above, there are the annual reports of the major philanthropic foundations, which provide very helpful information on the new developments in research programs, with frequent comments on areas of needed research.

INDEX

Academic research
amount of, in international relations, 12–19
attitudes toward, in international relations, 1–4, 24
authority and control over, 48–50
Access to foreign areas, problems of, 75–80
Access to materials, adaptations and improvisations needed to meet problem of, 89–92
Administrative aids to research, 45–50
Administrative setting for research, xiv–xv, 24–54
in large research centers, 40–45
Administrative support, importance of, in improving research skills, 19
Africa, 35, 96
as area study, 118, 119, 120
American Council of Learned Societies, 44
American Journal of International Law, 17, 94
American Political Science Association, v
programs devoted to research in international affairs, 17
American Political Science Review, 16, 94, 111–12
American Scholar, 94
American Universities Field Staff, 6
Annals of the American Academy of Political and Social Science, 94
Area studies
increased research in, 116–21
and multidisciplinary research, 70
Areas of needed research in international affairs, 122–29
Asia, 96
Asia Foundation, v

Barnes, Harry Elmer, 83
Beard, Charles A., 83
Book publishing for scholarly research, problem of, 99–103
Brazil, 39
Brookings Institution, 6
Seminars on American Foreign Policy, 35, 106, 114–15
Buenos Aires, 87
Burma, 77

Caribbean, 112
Carnegie, Andrew, 129
Carnegie Endowment for International Peace, v, vi, vii, viii, xiii, 6, 9, 24, 46, 94, 129
inventories of current research in international affairs, 110
Central files, governmental agency, gaps and losses in, 81–82
Central Intelligence Agency, 5, 105
Civil-military relations as subject of research, 121–22
Class schedules, needed changes in, 30–31
Committee for Economic Development, 6
Communism, effect of fear of, on research in international affairs, 86–87
Communist China, 52, 76, 86, 88
Core of courses versus "proprietary" course, 29–30
Council on Foreign Relations, 4, 83, 94, 110
Current History, 95
Cyprus, xi
Czechoslovakia, xi

Date, predetermined completion, for research undertaking, 57, 59–60
Department of Defense files, 84

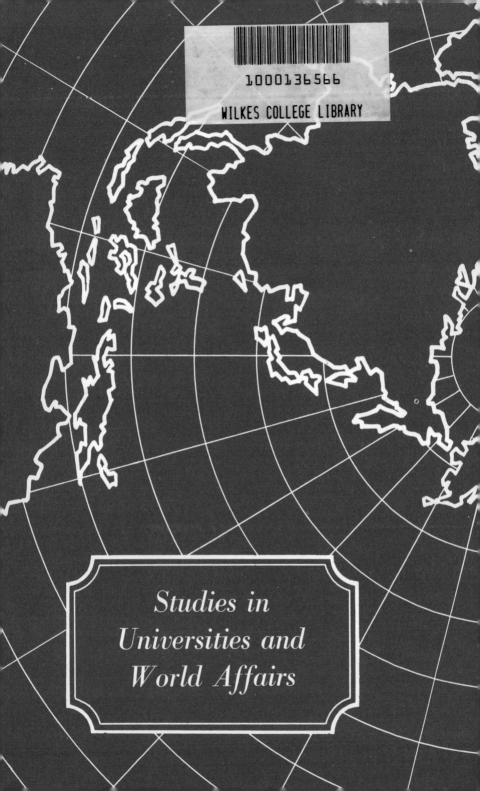

Studies in
Universities and
World Affairs